Charles Bray, Nelson Sizer

How to educate the Feelings or Affections

And bring the Dispositions, Aspirations, and Passions into Harmony with Sound

Intelligence and Morality

Charles Bray, Nelson Sizer

How to educate the Feelings or Affections
And bring the Dispositions, Aspirations, and Passions into Harmony with Sound Intelligence and Morality

ISBN/EAN: 9783337182359

Printed in Europe, USA, Canada, Australia, Japan

Cover: Foto ©ninafisch / pixelio.de

More available books at **www.hansebooks.com**

HOW TO EDUCATE

THE

FEELINGS OR AFFECTIONS,

AND

BRING THE DISPOSITIONS, ASPIRATIONS, AND PASSIONS INTO HARMONY WITH SOUND INTELLIGENCE AND MORALITY.

BY

CHARLES BRAY.

EDITED, WITH NOTES AND ILLUSTRATIONS

FROM THE THIRD LONDON EDITION,

BY

NELSON SIZER, OF NEW YORK,

AUTHOR OF "HOW TO TEACH;" "CHOICE OF PURSUITS," ETC., ETC.

NEW YORK:
S. R. WELLS & CO., PUBLISHERS,
737 BROADWAY.
1880.

CONTENTS.

SECTION I.

MENTAL CONSTITUTION, - - - - - - 17

SECTION II.

THE SELF-PROTECTING FEELINGS:

THE EDUCATION OF EACH FEELING CONSIDERED SEPARATELY.

ALIMENTIVENESS—APPETITE, - - - - - - 22
COMBATIVENESS, - - - - - - - - 30
DESTRUCTIVENESS, - - - - - - - - 37
SECRETIVENESS, - - - - - - - - 42
ACQUISITIVENESS, - - - - - - - - 50
CONSTRUCTIVENESS, - - - - - - - 55
CAUTIOUSNESS, - - - - - - - - - 59
LOVE OF LIFE, - - - - - - - - - 64

THE SELF-REGARDING FEELINGS:

SELF-ESTEEM, - - - - - - - - 66
LOVE OF APPROBATION, - - - - - - 71

THE SOCIAL AFFECTIONS:

AMATIVENESS, - - - - - - - - - 87
PHILOPROGENITIVENESS, - - - - - 91
ADHESIVENESS, - - - - - - - - 99

Contents.

THE MORAL FEELINGS:

  PAGE
- CONSCIENTIOUSNESS, - - - - - - - 103
- BENEVOLENCE, - - - - - - - - - 117
- CONSCIENTIOUSNESS AND BENEVOLENCE, - - - 120

THE ÆSTHETIC FEELINGS:

- IDEALITY, - - - - - - - - - 127

THE RELIGIOUS FEELINGS:

- VENERATION, - - - - - - - - - 134
- HOPE, - - - - - - - - - - 144
- SPIRITUALITY—WONDER, - - - - - - 149

FEELINGS WHICH GIVE CONCENTRATION, POWER, OR PERMANENCE TO THE OTHERS:

- CONCENTRATIVENESS AND INHABITIVENESS, - - - 154
- FIRMNESS, - - - - - - - - - 159
- IMITATION, - - - - - - - - - 165
- MIRTHFULNESS—THE FEELING OF THE LUDICROUS, - 169

- AUTHORITY AND OBEDIENCE, - - - - - - 176
- TEMPER, - - - - - - - - - 177
- PUNISHMENT, - - - - - - - - - 180
- MANNERS, - - - - - - - - - 183
- EXAMPLE, - - - - - - - - - 185

SECTION III.

THE CONNECTION OF MIND WITH ORGANIZATION. THE SUBJECTIVE AND THE OBJECTIVE, 191

SECTION IV.

- THE INTELLECTUAL FACULTIES, - - - - 205
- CONCLUSION, - - - - - - - - - 216

PREFACE

TO THE AMERICAN EDITION.

THE EDUCATION OF THE FEELINGS through the careful study of the brain was a field uncultivated previous to the discovery of Gall and Spurzheim. Several valuable treatises have since been given to the world in the endeavor to set forth the nature and action of all the mental powers, including the propensities, and how to lead them to automatic rectitude of action. Without an intimate acquaintance with every faculty, we can not hope to guide and regulate their forces. So long as the whole realm of passion is regarded by mankind, not as a set of faculties to be studied and governed, but as a single malign force, the inspiration of the prince of evil, or the inheritance of "total depravity," to be repressed by fear or uprooted by punishment, the passions, like volcanic fire, will continue to burn and consume their possessors, if they do not break forth into an open conflagration of crime. And thus the race goes on bemoaning crime, and helplessly exclaiming, "O Lord, how long?" Penalties may be enacted and severe punishment enforced by courts, but these do not touch the source of crime. So long as character depends on organization, and organization can be affected by training and habit, good and bad, reform can not be achieved by punishment, but must come from better culture, not of the intellect merely, but of the faculties which are concerned in passion or propensity, and in their abuse which leads to crime.

The importance of education can not be overestimated. Our pulpits, presses, and schools, which are the pride and blessing of our land, tend to show how much the race feels the need of improvement, and how much it is willing to do to raise from age to age the common level of human life. A moment's reflection will show that efforts in the direction of education have been mainly applied to the culture of the intellectual and moral feelings, while penalty and repression have been the chief means employed for the control of human passion and propensity. Men have become wise in science, able to master the great agencies of nature; but the turbulent passions within themselves have been little understood, except by the devastation and misery which have marked and marred the pathway of human progress and power.

A better day has dawned. The science of man is being studied, and ten thousand families, being discouraged in vain endeavor to control the propensities of their children, or to understand their own, are eagerly inquiring for the light which Phrenology would throw upon this first place of human need and human improvement.

Preface to the American Edition.

This work, by a countryman of George and Andrew Combe, is here presented as an aid in " The Education of the Feelings," and it has the special advantage of being based on a scientific analysis of the human faculties. Its expositions are so clear and plain that " the common people," without generous culture, yet anxious to train their children for honor and immortality, can understand and adopt its teachings.

The NOTES and ILLUSTRATIONS, it is hoped, will give additional interest to the text, and it is believed that the publishers are conferring a favor on their country by transferring from our fatherland a work so rich in possibility of benefit.

AMERICAN EDITOR.

PREFACE

TO LONDON EDITION.

EDUCATION has been correctly defined as the developing and perfecting of all our faculties. Without a definite and systematic knowledge of the human faculties, education in this sense is evidently impossible, and the time has arrived when, as a science, it must be inseparably blended with mental philosophy. Vague generalities ought no longer to be tolerated, but we ought to be able to state exactly what we wish to do—what we would have or not have: what feelings or intellectual faculties are, in individual cases, weak and require cherishing; what are too strong and require repressing; and what feelings especially we should wish to predominate in the character. The knowledge to guide us in these particulars is at present very vague and unsatisfactory, and based more upon custom and tradition than upon science. It is the aim of this work to give a more systematic direction to our inquiries in this department, and we have to ask the indulgence of our readers for the dry nomenclature which always attends, more or less, on attempts at classification.

With respect to the management of children, no very definite rules can be laid down, all children requiring different treatment according to the difference of their dispositions; and there is but one great rule invariably applicable—viz., to be ourselves what we would wish our children to be. Precept, without this, is comparatively useless; children's minds are fed and formed by the mental atmosphere which surrounds them; if we are selfish, they will become so too; if our morality and religion are little more than deference to public opinion, we must not expect that any higher feeling than love of applause will be developed under our guidance. We may more easily deceive ourselves in the knowledge of our own dispositions than we can deceive children, who, with their bright, intuitive vision, early learn to distinguish between truth and shams. So soon as children are intrusted to us, a kind of second education commences in ourselves: all that we say, do, and even feel, is imitated—we see the reflex of ourselves in others, and, startled into consciousness by the fac-simile, for the first time we begin to inquire what we are, and what we ought to be. In the course of our own early training, our immature powers were incapable of reflecting upon the nature of the different feelings which influenced us; but now, when we have to direct others, we feel that a correct analysis of the character is necessary. The object of the present volume is not so much to assist in the direct education of children, as in this second education of ourselves; to aid self-knowledge and self-development: or, if it were not thought too ambitious, we might say, that we aim at supplying a new system of moral philosophy, based upon an analysis of the use and abuse of each faculty, and its direction to its proper and legitimate objects.

If we would ascertain the purposes for which God has formed us, we must study the nature of the faculties with which He has endowed us, and make use of each faculty in the direction for which its nature shows it was evidently intended.

In our scheme, what Dr. Whewell calls *dependent* and *independent* morality, that is, the "intuitive" system and that based upon "utility," are blended, neither being able to act without the other. Thus we find in nature certain primitive impulses which make us wish to be kind to others; to respect and venerate whatever is great and good; and to do on all occasions what is right, irrespective of consequences, that is, at "whatever cost of pain and loss;" but these feelings, however strong, in no way indicate what is kind, or great and good, or right; of themselves they are mere blind impulses, as likely to go wrong as right, requiring, therefore, the direction of the reason. Reason requires a rule for its guidance, and all systems, even that of Dr. Whewell himself, are ultimately driven to "utility," or the "Greatest Happiness Principle," for this rule. It is, comparatively, of no use to feel the desire to do what is right, unless we know what *is* right, and it is of little use knowing what *is* right, without the desire to do it.

Mr. Buckle, in his surprising work on the History of Civilization, evidently confounds the knowledge of what is right with the desire to do it, that is, Moral

Principle with Moral Feeling; and because the first have undergone little change for the last three thousand years, he underrates the influence of moral *feeling* on the progress of Civilization. He says, "In reference to our moral conduct, there is not a single principle now known to the most cultivated Europeans, which was not likewise known to the ancients." This is very true, but the true progress of civilization is not marked by the progress of "opportunity," or by any "improvement in external circumstances," or by the mere knowledge of moral principles, but by our increased disposition to act in accordance with such principles. The far greater number of the actions of even the most reasonable, and almost all the actions of the mass of mankind, are what Hartley calls automatic, that is, involuntary—the product of feeling, not of intellect. Mr. Buckle says, "The child born in a civilized land is not likely, as such, to be superior to one born among barbarians; and the difference which ensues between the acts of the two children will be caused, so far as we know, solely by the pressure of external circumstances; by which I mean the surrounding opinions, knowledge, associations—in a word, the entire mental atmosphere in which the two children are respectively nurtured." Now this is altogether opposed to fact, and the source of this and of almost all of Mr. Buckle's errors of principle lies in his not giving sufficient importance to the fact of the connection of mind with organization, and to his appearing altogether to ignore what is equally proved, that the strength of mind both in thinking and feeling, is in proportion to the size and quality of the material organ with which it is connected; consequently, if the moral organs be small, moral feelings will be weak, and the moral manifestation or action will be weak in proportion, whatever the pressure of external circumstances or the mental atmosphere in which the child is nurtured. Mr. Buckle, however, admits "that it may be, owing to some physical causes still unknown, the average capacity of the brain is, if we compare long periods of time, becoming gradually greater; and that therefore the mind, which acts through the brain, is, even independently of education, increasing in aptitude and in the general competence of its views." "Such, however," he says, "is still our ignorance of physical laws, and so completely are we in the dark as to the circumstances which govern the hereditary transmission of character, temperament, and other personal peculiarities, that we must consider this alleged progress as a very doubtful point." We think, should Mr. Buckle's attention ever be turned to the discoveries of Gall and Spurzheim, he will find that they were not quite so much in the dark on this subject of hereditary tendencies as he appears to be; that the law for our guidance is, that exercise increases mental power and increases the size of the material organ, and that that increased size and *aptitude* are transmitted, not in "long periods of time," but from generation to generation, and that the advance of civilization is more properly measured by such increased mental power than by the "opportunities" and circumstances surrounding it.

THE EDUCATION
OF THE
FEELINGS, OR AFFECTIONS.

SECTION I.
MENTAL CONSTITUTION.

The education of the feelings, or formation of the dispositions, is a part of education which has been comparatively neglected; not so much because its importance has not been recognized, as because the too general want of definite knowledge concerning the affections and the moral springs of action has prevented its being pursued systematically.

The objection of this branch of education is the cultivation, by exercise, of those feelings which make us *wish* to do that which we *ought* to do. The mere knowledge of our duty, without the disposition to perform it, is of little use, or at most, but one small step gained; and yet, education, conducted as a system, has commonly stopped short at this point. Food is absolutely necessary to support life, but it is a question whether the mere knowledge of this would always be sufficient to induce us to take nourishment, if Nature had not endowed us with a strong desire to eat when requisite. The wants of our moral nature being less obtrusive, the laws which govern them are not so well understood; and yet it is equally certain that, with respect to religion and morality, that is, our duties to

God and our neighbor, the Creator has not been satisfied with merely telling us what we ought to do, but has also implanted feelings—such as love and reverence toward Himself, the moral sense, benevolence—which make us desire to perform the duties which His laws have pointed out to us. With this difference, that while the animal appetite is a full-grown instinct from the first, these incipient germs of our higher nature may, without watchful culture, lie undeveloped.

.The cultivation and training of the feelings bear the same relation to happiness, as the observance of the laws for the due regulation of the bodily system bear to health; and for the proper management of the feelings it is quite as necessary to know what they are, as it is to know the functions of the different organs of the body; and as important to treat each mental faculty separately, as to distinguish the heart from the lungs, the lungs from the liver; so that we may not apply our remedies to one organ when the disease is in another.

It is the province of mental philosophy to show what are the functions of the mind, to explain the manner in which they act, and their adaptation and relation to external objects. No such analysis of our mental constitution has been generally received, neither is it commonly understood that such is essential in education. But if education be a method of treatment of the mental faculties, how can it possibly be adapted to their direction unless we know the nature of these faculties, and their mode of action? Experience may have enlightened us a little here and there as to the best method of treating some of them; but the character of this knowledge has hitherto much resembled that of the quack practitioner, who having discovered a remedy for one disease, although ignorant of the nature of both remedy and disease, applies it to the cure of all. The little light that has been gained from experience, can never be properly systematized and applied to education, until the nature of our mental constitution be understood.

A parent is apt to think that the knowledge he possesses of his own disposition is sufficient for the guidance of the affections of his children; but dispositions differ so widely, that we can not have a falser guide, in many instances, than to judge of others by ourselves. The precept "know thyself," is very partially obeyed, and the knowledge of self which is attained is generally far too imperfect and indefinite to be applicable to the systematic training of the feelings.

Natural Philosophy has of late made rapid strides, and vastly augmented the power of man over the physical world; but because mankind have been unacquainted with the relation that such results bear to the nature of mind, education is very much in the condition it was before all this light shone upon us; consequently, the happiness of the world has not increased in a corresponding proportion with the multiplication of our comforts and conveniences.

The clearest analysis of the mental constitution, and the most practical, is that presented by Phrenology. This is admitted even by metaphysicians, who are not disposed equally to admit that each mental faculty is in connection with separate parts or organs of the brain.

Phrenology teaches, First: That the brain is the organ of mind.

Secondly: That it is not a single organ, but a congeries or bundle of organs, manifesting a plurality of faculties; and

Thirdly: That vigor of function bears a relation to the health, quality, and size of the organ.

It results from this that the mind and body are so intimately related, that it is quite impossible to separate moral from physical training. Nevertheless, the greater part of our remarks will be found applicable to the subject, independent of the truth of the phrenological propositions.

The mental constitution may be thus divided. The feelings consist of

THE SELF-PROTECTING.
ALIMENTIVENESS.
COMBATIVENESS.
DESTRUCTIVENESS.
SECRETIVENESS.
ACQUISITIVENESS.
CONSTRUCTIVENESS.
CAUTIOUSNESS.
THE LOVE OF LIFE.

THE SELF-REGARDING.
SELF-ESTEEM.
LOVE OF APPROBATION.

THE SOCIAL.
AMATIVENESS.
PHILOPROGENITIVENESS.
ADHESIVENESS.

THE MORAL.
CONSCIENTIOUSNESS.
BENEVOLENCE.

THE ÆSTHETIC.
IDEALITY.

THE RELIGIOUS.
VENERATION.
HOPE.
WONDER (OR SPIRITUALITY).

CONCENTRATIVENESS OR CONTINUITY.
FIRMNESS.
IMITATION.
} these faculties may furnish equal aid to all.

THE FEELING OF THE LUDICROUS (MIRTHFULNESS).

Of course it is not intended to assert that each of these faculties act separately in forming states of mind, but only that they constitute the principal ingredient—many of the other feelings necessarily mixing with them.

To these must be added the intellectual faculties, consisting of:

I.—THE EXTERNAL SENSES.
II.—THE PERCEPTIVE FACULTIES.
III.—THE REFLECTIVE.

I am sorry to use technical language which may be repulsive to some readers, but the terms must be considered as mere signs to which distinct ideas will be attached afterward. Every one possesses these faculties more or less developed, and their different combination in different persons constitutes the difference in individual character. Thus some are brave, some timid—some firm, others yielding—some proud, others modest, according as some faculty or group of faculties predominates.

Each feeling will be treated of separately, showing its use in the mental constitution, and also its abuse, so that in moral training we may know what to aim at, and what to avoid. The faculties will then be considered in groups, in order to appreciate the relative strength desirable for each to attain.

SECTION II.

THE EDUCATION OF EACH FEELING CONSIDERED SEPARATELY.

THE SELF-PROTECTING FEELINGS.

ALIMENTIVENESS—APPETITE.

APPETITE appears to belong more properly to physical than to moral education, but it bears too strongly upon the latter, both in its use and abuse, to be omitted here.

The pleasures of taste are among the first sensations that a child experiences; they assist essentially in forming the bond which unites it to the mother, its natural guardian and instructor; and from childhood to age, by their direct and reflected influence, add largely to the stock of human enjoyments. Let it not, therefore, be expected that children can be made to despise such pleasures; they can not, and they will not. Let us strive rather to give them a proper and healthy direction. The body must be fed and its waste repaired, or the mind can not maintain its vigor; and we have undoubted evidence that the intention of Nature with regard to man is that the lower propensities shall give impulse and strength to the higher. Indulgence of them beyond this point she does not fail to punish.*

---

* Alimentiveness is really the first mental element which comes into action, and, in the case of some idiots, seems to

JOSEPH HICKSON.
ALIMENTIVENESS.

PLATE II.

NOTE.—The Frontispiece will aid the reader in locating all the organs.

Alimentiveness. 23

Then let attention to this rule be a point of conscience with children. Eating is of the first importance, and so is the management and direction of the appetite, both as regards quantity and quality. As to quantity, children should be early taught to judge for themselves. Let them be instructed to discriminate between their feelings after a wholesome, moderate, but sufficient meal, and those which follow excess, either in quantity or quality. Let a feeling of shame and self-

---

be the only one ever awakened. The infant child or animal, at the beginning of conscious life, experiences the sense of hunger, and blindly, but instinctively seeks food. With the taking of food there is not only exquisite pleasure, but it supplies the necessary means of growth, and the recuperation of the system when it is exhausted by exercise. Hence the sense of hunger impels the eater to seek food at any cost of time and labor. Without the monitions of Alimentiveness in the form of appetite or hunger, men would be too busy with pleasure or profit to think of food, or to spend the time or money to procure it; and among the bad results would be an unhealthy irregularity in the taking of food both as to time and quantity, and illness and wasting of the system. We have known some persons who are so exceptionally deficient in the development of this propensity, that they forget to eat when much occupied with business. Finding themselves tired, weak, or faint, they have wondered what was the matter, until happening to think, or perhaps by the suggestion of a friend, they were reminded that they had not dined. Such men will carry a lunch to the forest or field and sometimes forget to eat it, or that they have it, until they pick up their things to go home. The Creator has wisely implanted this useful monitor in men and animals to insure the necessary supply of food, and has also kindly attached to its exercise the reward of exquisite gratification.

reproach be associated with the suffering which results from over-eating, or from improper food. Let them be commiserated for the wrong they have committed, not for its consequences; and let it be shown how future privation must follow present improper indulgence. It is better for them to learn thus to judge wisely for themselves, than be restricted to a certain allowance, which not even the most careful parent can at all times apportion to their real requirements. Nature will do this if her indications be attended to; and children must be taught to understand and obey them. Never let it be forgotten that in this, as in all cases, it is the object of education to teach a child to decide wisely for himself not only when under the control of parents and instructors, but in all circumstances, and in all places. Who has not admired the well-trained child, patiently waiting his turn to be served, however hungry he may be, quietly taking what is set before him; and although without any nursery mentor at his elbow, firmly resisting the temptation to gormandize and the injudicious kindness of "Oh, you *must* have a piece more! Only a little piece, there's a dear!" "This *can not* hurt you, I am sure!"

To insure a healthy appetite, children should enjoy fresh air, and bodily exercise in plenty; not only by regular walks out of doors, but by active cheerful play within; they should have a place appropriated to their use, where they may jump, and skip, and exhale the exuberance of their spirits, without annoyance to the sober members of the family. Their meals should be regular, and not too far apart; their diet nutritious, simple, but not too unvaried. A constant sameness of

Alimentiveness.

food sometimes produces a distaste which, of itself, causes a longing for forbidden food, arising from the craving of nature for variety. Within wholesome limits it is desirable that their palates should be gratified in the choice of food for them; their inclinations will not then be so readily excited to improper indulgence. A child should be allowed to eat only at meal-times, with very slight exceptions, which a sensible mother will know how to make; such as giving a piece of bread to divide the time between breakfast and dinner, if it be too long. How frequently do we see this rule, one of the simplest for the preservation of health, broken, and digestion continually disturbed by the introduction of fresh food! A child cries—it is pacified with something eatable. Sometimes the child, more sensible than its nurse, turns away its head, and resists the unseasonable offer, until coaxed into overcoming its natural reluctance—" because it is *so* nice."

A common practice seems to be to make the enjoyment of eating the grand ultimatum. It is held out as the strongest inducement to "behave well;" it is the promised reward of obedience; it is the convenient resource of the nurse "to keep the child quiet;" it is the bribe of the friendly visitor to gain the child's attention; it must furnish occupation to the child when its restless attempts to acquire a knowledge of things around it are troublesome. The very infant's tears are assuaged by anticipations of the "nice pudding" that is coming; its own impatience is heightened by the affected impatience of the nurse, who excites instead of allaying the eagerness for selfish gratification. If in addition to all this, children continually see their elders taking anxious "thought what they shall eat, and what they shall drink," can it be wondered at, that they should over-rate the importance of the pleasures of appetite, and that such lessons should be seldom unlearned in after-life?

Sweetmeats and other delicacies are indeed a common reward for the good deeds, and the denial of them a common punishment for the sins of childhood. The mischief arising from this is not only the training of children to be gluttons and epicures, which it must infallibly do by making the gratification of the palate of such paramount importance; but a greater evil is to be dreaded—the weakening of the moral sense by supplying an unworthy and temporary motive to obedience when a higher one alone can be adequate and permanent. An example may illustrate this. " Mrs. —— was very anxious (as every right-minded mother must be) that her child should be religious, and no pains were spared to make him so, as will appear. The boy (not four years old) was brought down to dessert. In due course the nurse came in to take him to bed, when this conversation took place : Mamma.—' Say your prayers, my darling.' Boy.—' I won't.' M.—' Oh, yes—now *be* good. Show Miss such-an-one how prettily you can say your prayers.' (Silent, pouting lips). M.—' Come now, you don't know what grandmamma has for you.' Boy.—' What?' M.—' An orange.' Grandmamma.—' There's Shamrock (the dog) now, make haste, or we'll get Shamrock to say pretty prayers.' M.—' Yes, dear, now do—because of the orange, you know.' Will it be believed that this chattering had the desired effect upon the boy? Worked upon by greediness and vanity, he lisped the Lord's Prayer in a sulky, muttering manner, was called a good boy, and went to bed, but *without the orange.* When he asked for it, 'to-morrow' was the answer. Here were lessons in plenty; here, in five minutes, were inculcated impressively greediness, stupid surrender of the understanding, vanity, lying, and hypocrisy."* Lessons—little needed, for where from original constitution or from early mismanagement the selfish feelings are strong, they will produce such fruits in abundance, unless counteracted by assiduous moral culture. The constant recurrence of the temptations to the abuse of appetite, render it in such cases difficult to manage, but that well-educated children can and do control it by opposing to it the moral feelings is daily proved. Dr. Johnson describes "politeness" as consisting in giving no preference to oneself; and I have seen a child choose the smallest orange, the least rosy apple, the most uninviting corner of cake, and leave for his companions the nicest piece, the finest fruit—and this unconscious of any observing eye.

It is much to be doubted whether very young children, under the age of five or six, should be obliged to keep silence at meals, and not ask for what they want. "Sit still; do not ask, and you will have what is proper for you," is very well at a more advanced age, when children are able to judge of and appreciate the propriety and justice of such restrictions as applied only to themselves and not to those about them. In young children let everything be expressed, let the mind be

---

* Monthly Repository.

clear as crystal. What they shall eat is necessarily an object of great interest to children, and they look with eagerness and longing curiosity on the dishes before them. Let the child say his wish aloud, and by your immediate refusal or acquiescence, put him out of all suspense about it as soon as possible. It is much easier to refuse what is improper at once than afterward, when you know the child has been many minutes looking and longing; a refusal then frequently excites a sense of injury and injustice which, had it been given at first and at once, it would not have done. Such refusals, however, should be as few as possible, as it is impossible to prevent children from considering it an "undue preference" for grown-up people to indulge in that which is denied to themselves, and thus early imbibing a lesson in selfishness.* Much more attention is due to dieting, that is, to a varied and whole-

---

* If parents would refrain from having on the table articles of food which are improper for children it would be better for themselves, and save a world of trouble. It would doubtless be better for parents to use nothing as food or drink which would be injurious to children ten years old. Then daily habit, and the example of parents, would combine to establish in children usages in respect to appetite which would become as second nature. The cakes, candies and sweetmeats, which not a few parents permit children to eat, lay the foundation for nine-tenths of the sickness and death which are the terror and scourge of most families. The children of poverty who are obliged to live plainly, and to go barefoot and half clad, playing in the dirt and getting tanned in sunshine and wind, seem to be healthy, not because dirt and raggedness are sanitary blessings, but because their food is coarse and plain, and

some food, in proper quantities, than is ordinarily paid; and when we consider how much the benevolent designs of Nature are frustrated in the perversion of this eating propensity, the waste of life, and happiness, and the amount of suffering it occasions, we may be held excused for dwelling so long upon its due exercise and restraint. Dr. William Sweetzer judiciously observes, that there exists a corresponding action between the moral feelings and the *viscera;* that the particular condition of the former may either determine, or be determined by, that of the latter. Indigestion, for example, is well known to be sometimes the consequence, and sometimes the cause, of an irritable and unhappy temper. A sour disposition may either occasion, or result from a sour stomach. Thus, in some instances, we sweeten the stomach by neutralizing the acerbity of the temper, while in others we sweeten the temper by neutralizing the acidity of the stomach. Who has not felt his digestion improve under the brightening of his moral feelings? And who has not experienced the brightening of his moral feelings under the improvement of his digestion? The reason will now be manifest why those children who are so unfortunate as to be indulged with cakes, pastry, sweetmeats, and the like indigestible articles, other

---

the sunshine and air, with free exercise, give them constitutions, which the rich would gladly give tens of thousands to have transferred to their children. In despair they cry, why do these rough children of poverty live, and our favorites of fortune, with culture and distinction before them, fade and die? Physiology and common sense, strangers often to wealth and pride, would answer.

things being the same, require reproof or the rod so much oftener than those who are restricted to more plain and wholesome food. Indeed, an exclusive diet of bread and milk, united with judicious exercise in the open air, will often prove the most effectual means of correcting the temper of peevish and refractory children.

The loss, physical and mental, resulting from the absurd habit of society with respect to the table ; by the three courses, and late dinners—the over-eating and drinking—will, perhaps, be better considered after it is determined what a man ought to be when all his higher powers are fully trained and developed.

COMBATIVENESS.

This feeling supplies natural or physical courage, but the word Oppositiveness, perhaps, better points out the inherent feeling to which the above term is applied, namely, the opposition which rises in the mind when any obstacle to its desires presents itself. The world is full of difficulties and dangers, and the pathway to all that is really excellent is often so beset with obstacles, that in addition to moral courage and intellectual force, an instinct to do battle—a pleasure in overcoming difficulties for its own sake, irrespective of the end to be attained, has been added. The attitude of defiance which the mind assumes by means of this faculty, harmonizes it, so to speak, with a rugged and difficult world. The feeling then requires directing rather

EZRA CORNELL.

COMBATIVENESS.

PLATE III.

than restraining. The judicious educator will not be so anxious to check the disposition to contend, as to provide it with a legitimate field of action; he will endeavor so to interest the other feelings and the intellect in pursuits high and excellent, and the whole force of the combative propensity may be brought to bear on the difficulties which must necessarily be encountered. In early childhood the deficiency of Oppositiveness is felt to be a happy circumstance; the child is docile and tractable, takes a suggestion immediately, does as he is bidden, has no will of his own. Cause for congratulation, however, lessens every year. The least trifles discourage; at lesson-time you are wearied with the constant whining, "I can't do it;" and at play-time you are mortified to see one pursuit after another abandoned at the slightest difficulty. The boy lacks courage and manly spirit to encounter and overcome.

The love of contention and opposition for their own sake constitutes the abuse of the faculty; the proper management of it, therefore, when in excess, evidently consists in exciting its direct manifestation as little as possible. By the force of sympathy, the manifestation of Combativeness in one person immediately arouses the feeling in another; in children especially, the outward expression from another's mind is reflected as in a mirror. In seeking to correct a child this fact should never be lost sight of. If our tone be harsh and captious, the child's feelings will be arrayed against the reproof, instead of being softened into contrition. "You are *so quoss!*" a little boy, pouting, said to his mother, who asked him to do something which did not fall in with his humor at the time. "Am I cross?" replied she, in a tone the perfection of sweetness and gentleness. The child's temper melted immediately, and he stood silent and abashed under the sense of his own unreasonableness. On the other hand, the reflection from our own Combativeness is so instantaneous, that it is sometimes hard to say on which side the discipline is first and most needed. A mother sees her child doing something wrong; in a sharp, angry tone she commands him to desist immediately. The child's disposition to oppose is roused by the tone of the reproof, and he still persists; upon which the mother repeats the command still more sharply—perhaps adding a threat by way of enforcing it. But this also is disregarded, as is every succeeding attempt to procure obedience, because the child's Combativeness is sure to be excited in proportion to that of the mother. The warfare perhaps terminates by the mother giving way first, while she satisfies her conscience by declaring that "Papa shall know all about it when he comes home, and will be sure to punish you," thus showing very evidently her own incapacity, and making papa a bugbear. If, as is often the case, the mother magnanimously perseveres, enforces obedience, and punishes the resistance, almost equal mischief is done. While she is exulting within herself upon her proper display of authority, and boasting that she knows how to manage her children with firmness, she little thinks that by her own injudicious conduct she herself was the cause of disobedience in her child; and that instead of having gained, she has lost considerable authority by having lost much in the child's esteem and affection. He will do the same thing again when his mother is not present, because he has no motive but fear to deter him.

A child never fails to perceive if the punishment be inflicted in a spirit of Combativeness or in sorrow and affection, and the remembrance of this, when calmness is restored, makes the whole difference as to whether the fruits of the lesson be good or evil. If, however, in the first instance, the mother had laid down her command in a perfectly kind, gentle, yet firm manner, the child must have been ill-trained beforehand if he did not obey immediately. Even without positive harshness, there is often an indescribable something in our manner or intonation which never fails to excite rebellion. Some teachers of good sense and quick sympathy have excellent tact in perceiving to a nicety the tone which will insure obedience; to others this perception could never be conveyed, owing to certain deficiencies in their own organization, and these persons are often puzzled to account for their lack of power. We smile at the lamentable ignorance of cause and effect on the part of the poor uncultivated mother who has no remedy for the rebelliousness of her young urchins but a box on the ear; but the utter want of tact and common sense is often as obvious in many a polished lady, who attempts to correct her child in most elegant language, but with a manner and emphasis irritating to the last degree. It is to be feared that the Golden Rule is not much heeded in the management of our children, as there is mostly a lurking persuasion, when the two wills come into collision, that it is theirs to endure, and ours to inflict; otherwise the precept, "Do as you would be done by," would throw light on many a dilemma of this kind, and suggest the right course in multitudes of cases where no other general rule can be applied. Put yourself as much as possible in your child's place. Picture to yourself the kind of admonition that would have the most power over your own mind, the tone of voice and manner that would least excite passion and rouse opposition, and adopt that. Do not attempt to drive, but always to lead. When a child is interested in some object of his own, do not, by a sudden command, interfere with it, but rather allow him a few minutes' grace, and gradually divert his attention from one thing to another. Do not unnecessarily thwart your children in their little objects; for however insignificant they may appear to you, they are all-important to them, and pursued with proportionate eagerness. The temper of no child is proof, or ought to be proof, against the frequent, useless intermeddling of some parents and nurses, by whom he is allowed to bring nothing to an end, and obliged to relinquish all his little projects uncompleted. The more a child possesses of the spirit of opposition, the more uniformly kind and considerate should its instructors endeavor to be.

When strong, and joined to great Self-esteem, this feeling becomes very difficult to manage either in ourselves or children. It then begets almost an unconscious habit of opposition to all that is either suggested or proposed by other people. Everything must originate with self, or it is ignored and put down at once. It may be even so strong and unreasonable as to give the idea that the desire to contend comes from other people and not from ourselves, as in the Scotsman, who, upon a friend mildly suggesting that it was a fine day, immediately rejoined: "And wha said anything against the day, I'd like to know; you'd quarrel with a stone wa'." I have seen a person with the feeling so strong as to induce him to put down a statement as untrue from another which he himself had made only an hour before, but for the moment had forgotten that it had originally come from himself. The most important thing to be inculcated in the direction of this faculty is, that it should never be exercised but in connection with the sense of duty, and so indissoluble should be the association between them, that the disposition to contend and dispute should never arise without the voice of conscience urging the question: "Is it consistent with the rights of others, with truth and justice, to contest this point?"*

The minds of many persons are kept in a continual ferment by the predominance of this feeling, together with Self-esteem, which leads them even to resent as an offense on the part of others conduct in which not the slightest offense was intended. At a single word

---

* A suggestion, with quarrelsome and obstinate persons, is better than a command. A gentle little girl will manage a big, rough brother, better than one can who is like himself though he were twice as large. The liberty of choosing the good or the bad way of doing, throws the child upon his honor to do rightly, while a positive command or absolute interdiction may provoke him to do wrong on purpose, so as not to seem cowardly or submissive. A low, firm tone makes a gentle mother's word law to her fiery, grown-up son, when the angry, domineering threat of the father would be defied, though disobedience might result in a disinheriting quarrel.

construed by them into an indignity, or into a disposition to injure them, the feeling is in arms, all comfort and equanimity of temper is destroyed, and the unhappy individual suffers far more, mentally, than he could have done from the offense, had it been real instead of imaginary.

But we must not only control and guide the feeling, but where it is deficient take means to stimulate and strengthen it, for it is almost impossible to attain eminence in any active direction in the world without it. Constantly encourage the child to meet and overcome obstacles without your aid, and never let him rest satisfied to leave anything half-finished. Dangers and difficulties must be daily created. Riding, climbing, and for some children even shooting and hunting may be resorted to for this purpose. We must not hide danger, or always guard children from it by our own power and experience, but teach them to meet it boldly. Let them know the consequences to be incurred, and the pain to be borne, and teach them to bear it. Courage consists in meeting danger, not in blindly overlooking it. The most mischievous results may often be witnessed from surrounding children—boys especially—from their earliest infancy, with those whose duty is made to consist in doing everything for them, in guarding them from every little danger and inconvenience, clearing every path from obstruction, and constantly coddling and waiting upon them, instead of teaching them to meet and overcome all their little difficulties themselves, and occasionally helping them to do so. Under such mistaken kindness, this faculty frequently becomes paralyzed; and all is done that can be done to make of a child a puny, puling, weak, effeminate character.

DESTRUCTIVENESS.

Nature bestows no qualities that are not intended to conduce to the good of the individual and to his fellow-beings. The endowment of Destructiveness, although most mischievous in its abuse, in its right application is highly necessary and useful. It is supposed to give the inclination to destroy; in its abuse, it is the desire of inflicting pain for the sake of giving pain, that is, cruelty.

The feeling in its proper state helps to produce energy of character, indignation against wrong, and resolution to inflict *necessary* pain; but uncontrolled by the moral faculties, it becomes anger, passion, revenge, cruelty, the love of tormenting.

These latter manifestations of Destructiveness often make their appearance very early. Some young children have a strange propensity to torture and kill flies and other little animals within their reach, which propensity entirely disappears in after-life, when other feelings have combined to temper the pure destructive instinct. It is obviously expedient never to excite the faculty by allowing a child to witness any act of destruction whatever; as little as possible to make allusion to killing and cruelty of any kind; and always to avoid associating the animal food eaten at table with the lambs, pigs, or poultry he meets with in his daily walks. If we must be devourers of our fellow-creatures, let us keep our cannibalism in the background as much as possible.

The charge of favorite animals will have the best tendency to counteract the propensity, by creating a habit of kindly feeling toward living creatures. If parents or teachers have unfortunately a constitutional repugnance toward some species of animals, they will do well to conceal it, and, like a lady of our acquaintance, allow their lap to be filled with black beetles rather than communicate a shudder of disgust; since the feelings of dislike and fear in young children are often accompanied by those of anger and cruelty, although they may not be in ourselves.

The expression of this feeling in petty revenge is often foolishly encouraged by nurses, "Did the naughty stick fall down and hurt baby?—*beat* naughty stick!" and even if a brother or sister are the offenders, the same amiable spirit of retaliation is impressed. A lady once trod inadvertently on the toes of a little cherub-faced girl; she pursued her like a fury, and would not be appeased till she had stamped on her toes in return. The natural tendency of this feeling is an eye for an eye, and a tooth for a tooth. Parents themselves frequently punish their children on the same principle for an involuntary error, provided its consequences are vexatious to themselves. The tone of correction in general partakes too much of passion and the spirit of revenge rather than of sorrow and of love. While this is the case, we can not expect children to learn to subdue the irritation of temper they feel when anything displeases them, and the habit once formed of giving way to it will be most difficult of subjection in after-

GEN. ISRAEL PUTNAM.

DESTRUCTIVENESS.

PLATE IV.

life. When united with an excess of this feeling there is a considerable love of opposition in a child, the temper becomes extremely difficult to manage, and perhaps the only way to succeed is to avoid as much as possible all occasions of exciting it, so that the feeling may decrease for want of exercise; while at the same time we cultivate diligently the moral and reasoning powers to oppose it. Even in the cradle the discipline should be begun; everything that is liable to excite the temper, to rouse the irascible feelings, should as far as possible be avoided, and when once excited, instead of leaving the child to cry and wear its passion out, its attention should be diverted and its feelings changed. From want of proper caution in small instances like this, a child frequently commences life with a bias in the temper and disposition not easily to be remedied.

Sometimes, when the outward burst of passion is conquered, the feeling which dictates it finds vent in spiteful actions or ill-natured words; in more advanced life, in bitter sarcasm or cutting innuendoes. Let the young be taught, that the amount of pain which is given to others under the influence of such a feeling is the measure of the offense thus committed, whatever may be the tone or gesture that accompanies it.

The love of mischief seems to arise partly from this propensity and partly from the want of proper occupation for a restless, active spirit. Let children have a plenty of useful and innocent employment found for them, and they will not be so fond of exercising their faculties to the destruction of things around them.

The feeling, like all others, is most readily caught from sympathy. An atmosphere of passion and destructive feeling may be created, as we have seen ; and an ordinarily mild, kind, and polite people, breathing and stimulated by such an atmosphere, may become cruel and ferocious and live in a sea of blood. Benevolence, kindness, justice, best control this faculty.*

What is usually called Temper results from this feeling, and the way in which it arises or shows itself afterward, depends upon the other feelings with which it may be combined, and which may predominate in the disposition. With some, anger is a sudden outburst

---

* Too much dictation in respect to every little thing irritates the Destructiveness of a child and makes it abnormal in size and activity. We met a little girl not four years old with the organ enormously developed. Neither of the parents had it more than medium, and a younger sister had it but moderate, in size. On asking the history of the case, the mother in sorrow, said, she was herself to blame for the terrible temper of the child. She resolved, having seen much bad training in families, to train her child perfectly and make it behave. Hence every infantile act, not in accordance with decorous propriety, was taken notice of. Things a babe might not touch were left in her way and her hands were whipped if she touched them, and in every possible way she was snubbed and her temper kept sour ; was called naughty, her faults repeated to friends and made the most of, so as to impress their enormity on her mind. Then she grew worse, until the mother said, " Talking and whipping do no good; she flies at me and her baby sister in a wild frenzy of passion and I fear she will yet commit murder." The younger child had been treated differently, and its Destructiveness not excited, and the organ had remained in harmony and proper keeping with the other faculties.

and soon over, and is quickly succeeded by the wish to make amends for the pain it may have given, or the mischief it may have wrought in its raging. This is where respect and kindness, and, above all, Conscientiousness predominate in the character, and where there is an absence of Concentrativeness, Secretiveness, and Cautiousness. In others, anger burns internally, and is vindictive, sulky, and lasting; in this case the latter feelings, together with pride, are in excess, and the former frequently deficient. But Conscientiousness is the great desideratum in every character, and tends above all to keep every other feeling in its proper place and bounds. It is this that—whether we are open or sullen, forgiving or vindictive, whether our anger be transient or lasting—always ultimately brings us back into the right path and desire " to do only as we would be done by:" and there are some people that we rather like than otherwise to see angry, because we know that when the fit is over, and their conscience begins to call them to task, they will be overflowing for some time to come in every good and kind and generous feeling. I have known some naughty boys take advantage of this reaction of feeling, and get a flogging on account, well knowing that they could get almost anything they chose to ask afterward. Destructiveness without Benevolence leads to great severity. Old soldiers describe the *furor* that comes over them in battle—the maddened, blood-shot eye, the love of blood, and delight in killing for its own sake. But this delight in blood is an abuse, not the proper use, of an otherwise necessary feeling.

SECRETIVENESS.

The mind requires a covering as much as the body, and this faculty, properly exercised, furnishes the desire to conceal thoughts and feelings which are better not exposed. It is true "that the truth must not be told at all times," that true wisdom and benevolence often forbid the utterance of the thought which is in our minds; that it is better to suppress certain feelings or ideas than by publishing them to give useless pain to others; but, however valuable Secretiveness, or the tendency to conceal, may be in matured life, as assisting in the formation of proper reserve, prudence, and that "better part of valor—discretion;" the instinct requires less notice in early childhood with respect to its use than its abuse.

It is necessary clearly to comprehend the young mind in all its inmost workings as well as outward manifestations, in order to direct it aright. A child should, therefore, repose unlimited confidence in one or both of his parents; and that he may be encouraged to this, fear should be banished from the intercourse; the child should learn to look upon them as sympathizing friends who will enter into all his feelings and enjoyments, and to whom he may freely communicate his thoughts upon all occasions. They will thus be able to give the right direction to the feelings and propensities, and uproot error before its growth shall have injured, as all error must do, the truths already planted. It is scarcely credible to those who have not minutely observed it, to what a train of errors *one* false perception will give rise in the mind of a child. A French author justly observes on this subject, "Error, dangerous in

M. SOMNEILLER.

SECRETIVENESS.

PLATE V.

itself, is still more so by propagation: one produces many. Every man compares more or less his ideas together. If he adopt a false idea, that united with others produces such as are necessarily false, which combining again with all those which his memory contains, gives to all of them a greater or less tinge of falsehood." Again he says, "A single error is sufficient to degrade a people, to obscure the whole horizon of their ideas." These errors can only be properly removed at their source, which is not easily discovered unless children are in the habit of confiding closely in their instructor; if he be a judicious one he will not despise their little ideas, nor ridicule their mistakes or simple misapprehensions.

A child who was very literal in his ideas, had often heard the passage of Scripture read, "Even the very hairs of your head are all numbered," and received from it the idea, that a figure denoting its particular number was inscribed on each hair. One day his brothers and sisters were amusing themselves with a microscope, and called him eagerly to look through it at a few hairs placed underneath. He looked at it earnestly for some time, and then muttered, "I don't see the number!" His companions laughed at the absurdity of his exclamation. He was abashed at their laughter and did not explain, but the idea remained in his mind that the Bible had said something that was not true.

It is the mistaken idea of some parents that in order to secure the confidence of their children, they must assume a sort of infallibility, and must never let it be found out that their own knowledge is at fault. When, therefore, they are taxed with questions that they can not answer, they evade them by such prevarications as "Want of time just then to attend to them,"—"Not a proper question to be asked,"—"Beyond a child's capacity to understand,"—and so on. Such parents little think how much they undermine confidence by this and every species of shuffling, which children are sure to detect and almost as sure to imitate. It is their duty to qualify themselves in every possible way for satisfying the desire for knowledge in their children; but if they can not, let them simply and honestly confess their ignorance, and become fellow-learners with their children to find an answer, if the question is worth answering. A half-educated mother, who does not pretend to more knowledge than she really has, but who has the wish for more, commands much more the respect and confidence of her children than if her learning and acquirements were the fullest possible, because they know what she professes to know, she really does know, and because it is the instinct of humanity from childhood upward to respect and confide in truth and honesty far more than in extent of knowledge. It is the same with moral deficiencies. Parents know that they ought to be models for their offspring, and sometimes, therefore, wish it to be assumed that they are so, and tacitly forbid their own weaknesses being made subject of comment before the children. The little creatures, however, make comments enough about them among themselves, and, perhaps, learn that hypocrisy is a grace for the drawing-room, and truth a luxury for the nursery. Perfect candor toward our children with respect to our own failings—showing that we earnestly desire to correct them if we can, and if we can not, using them as a warning for their benefit—is the best possible way of making them candid and above disguise in return. If we really seek the good of our children and not our glorification, in many cases the precept, "Confess your faults one to another," may be acted upon even between parents and children in preference to the adoption of any one-sided confessional.

Where real confidence exists between parents and their child, there is little danger to be apprehended even from a naturally secretive disposition, because the parents will be able to see its workings, and counteract them where they are tending to evil. They will encourage, by leniency, the confession of faults, and prove to the offender that openness is more advantageous than concealment. When a child with such a disposition is treated with severity or indifference, when his thoughts and feelings, if he does utter them, are disregarded, when the avowal of a fault draws down the chastisement instead of averting it, what can we expect but that he should use cunning to attain his wishes, and falsehood to evade punishment? If deceit and lying be made his interest, he will practice them.

The summary modes of punishment still in frequent use, such as corporal punishment, solitary confinement, or tasks for all species of misconduct, have a strong tendency to call the propensity we are speaking of into exercise. Children, not seeing the connection between the penalty and the offense, naturally enough conclude, that to avoid the penalty they have only to conceal the offense. The proper punishment for a fault, which God himself has appointed for us, is the natural consequences of the error. We should, therefore, in order to correct a fault, allow these natural consequences to fall upon the child, who will thus generally see the connection between them, and abstain from its commission in future; but when these consequences are not plainly discernible, or are too remote to operate sufficiently, the punishment should have reference to the offense. For example, he is permitted to play in a garden upon condition that he willfully damages nothing; he tramples down the young and tender plants to reach the unripe fruit, which he plucks—the natural consequence is the loss of the flowers and fruit in their season. But he has also broken the conditions on which he was admitted—the punishment for this is exclusion from the privilege, until a sincere conviction of his error vouches for his better fulfillment of the condition. Or, in a fit of passion, he may have hurt or injured his companions —the natural punishment is the being left by them until the state of mind which induced the commission of the fault is changed, and he seeks their society and forgiveness sensible of his own error in alienating those whose companionship is necessary to his happiness. The only proper and effectual remedy for error is to show why it is error, and to excite the desire to correct it; merely to forbid it under certain penalties, without this conviction of the understanding, rather induces the child to commit it, when he can do so with impunity.

As motives to obedience, the selfish feelings should be appealed to as little as possible, even in early childhood; and when the moral feelings have been cultivated and strengthened, not in any case. Thus we should not appeal to a child's appetite, or his fear, to his desire of applause, or pride; but to his sense of right, his desire to make us happy, his love and veneration for God, from whom, as he may soon be taught to perceive, all his enjoyments proceed.

While we deprecate most earnestly the abuse of the faculty under notice, we must not forget entirely its use, even in childhood. Under the guidance of the moral powers, it gives rise to some valuable qualities of mind; to a prudent reserve, and, in after-life, to a judicious tact and management, to a proper regard for time, place, and circumstance. It will put a bridle on the tongue, and enable us to conceal those feelings which the deceit or selfishness of others would take advantage of—for we must not "wear our heart upon our sleeves, for daws to peck at." Children under this influence will suppress the outward indication of the selfish feelings, that they may not interfere with the enjoyment of others. They will bear pain without complaining, that they may not give pain to those around them; they will prefer to keep their uneasy sensations to themselves, rather than oblige everybody near to participate in them. They will be modest and unobtrusive, not demanding for their ideas, their concerns, first attention, but repressing their impatience until their turn for notice arrives.

An open, frank, ingenuous disposition is the most lovely of all, and that to which we can the soonest attach ourselves; but it does not always follow that a child of reserved temper is disingenuous; love of truth, candor of spirit, and a warm, affectionate disposition may dwell under the natural reserve. Kindness and trust will cherish and draw forth the best feelings of such a nature, while severity and suspicion will act upon it with most baneful influence.

We should always avoid all double dealing, or even double meaning. Let us never make any profession before children which we do not mean—profess, for instance, to be glad to see people whom we are not glad to see, and whom immediately before we were speaking against. If we ever wear two faces, children will soon learn to imitate us.

The love of truth and candor can never be cultivated with success while children see a disregard of it in others. If it were universal, if the light of truth were permitted to shine upon our characters and conduct, how much better should we feel ourselves obliged to be, what a different race should we become! Thousands of actions which are now performed because we think no one sees them or will find out the motives that induced them, would be replaced by such as would bear the daylight. A sound writer observes: "There is nothing that we ought to reject with more unalterable firmness than an action that, by its consequences, reduces us to the necessity of duplicity and concealment. No man can be eminently respectable, or amiable, or useful, who is not distinguished for the frankness and candor of his manners. This is the grand fascination by which we lay hold of the hearts of our neighbors, conciliate their attention, and render virtue an irresistible object of imitation."

There are two classes of character with which we are all familiar—those whose feelings and emotions may all be said to go on outside of them, and those who keep all their thoughts and feelings to themselves. This openness or reserve depends very much upon the strength of this faculty and its combination with Cautiousness and Approbativeness; and the whole character, and particularly the way in which it affects others, very much turns upon the proportion of Secretiveness in it. Under the influence of this combination, every other feeling expresses itself with a distinctive difference; and however alike in opinion and principle persons may be in whom this difference exists, this similarity is little apparent. We are drawn at once to the frank, candid, open-hearted person, but our love is more lasting for the prudently reserved. We dislike loud expression even where the virtues are alone concerned, and the reserved person is much less likely to offend in all other respects than the open one. We place the clear light of truth to be desired above everything, but the close person will frequently find his account in his reserve, as the world often gives credit for sense where there is only silence, and believes a well to be deep when it is only dark. Strong Hope with this feeling weak, leads to great loquacity, and often betrays shortcomings against which there would be no other than this self-witness.*

---

*A proper endowment of Secretiveness, with justice and good sense, leads a person not to repeat what others may say, if the effect of its circulation would harm any person in mind, body, character, standing, or estate. The gossiper is not necessarily a bad meaning person, though his tongue is like a torch setting society on fire and plucking down a hornet's nest about his own ears, and that of all of whom he speaks. People are not perfect—especially *other* people—and no one is free from ways, words, surroundings, or characteristics which may not be criticised, found fault

ACQUISITIVENESS.

The love of acquisition is so widely spread in the world, that, as in the case of the last-mentioned faculty, there is far less occasion to advert to its use, than to its abuse. We *must* accumulate to provide against want, both for our own sakes and for that of our offspring, who for years are unable to provide for themselves—and this is its use; but to its almost universal abuse, and to the want, in general, of clear ideas as to the nature of real happiness, as a result of the misuse of property when acquired, are owing many of the prevalent evils of society at the present day.

---

with, or ridiculed. And what is the good of it? Do we do it to show our wisdom, culture, or fortunate condition, in contrast with theirs? If so, it is mean and egotistical. If to depress and scourge others for what in part they may not be to blame, it is detestable. Many seem to have a "mouth like an open sepulchre" full of the bones of slaughtered victims. Their tongue is not only fiery and bitter, but it is too noisy, always carelessly, if not malignly, busy. Such persons soon become feared and avoided. What they say to be sociable and friendly, and place themselves high by flattering the present and scoring the absent, defeats its object, by making every listener afraid to say a word which means anything, or to be friendly or even pleasant and sociable. Speak evil of none carelessly. The Quaker lady was right in her way. Her daughter told a friend who was visiting her that her mother, she believed, would speak well even of the devil, if he were slandered in her presence. When she re-entered the room, the visitor said, "Thy daughter says she thinks thee would take the devil's part if he were slandered in thy presence." She instantly replied with a smile, "We might all profitably imitate his industry and perseverance."

B. H. BRISTOW.

ACQUISITIVENESS.

PLATE VI.

We have passed from a military to a commercial age, and the aims of the one are pursued in almost the same unreasoning spirit as those of the other. The general crusade in pursuit of wealth is almost as mad as was that for the recovery of the Holy Sepulchre. The spirit of gain has seized the whole population; and accumulation for its own sake, or for the sake of mere animal indulgence and of the most absurd, paltry, and vain distinctions, is widely prevalent.

Boys are too frequently brought up to consider the acquirement of property as almost the chief end and aim of their existence; and if not the letter, this is at least the spirit of the instructions they receive: business must be attended to before everything else, and all other duties are to give place to it. In this faculty we have an illustration of what *may* be done in the cultivation and strengthening of the feelings, for we continually meet with instances in which it has become so strong by constant action that the whole life is spent in its exercise, from the mere love of acquiring, without reference to the end for which acquisition is made. More frequently, however, persons amass all they can with the object of purchasing with it, not rational enjoyment, but what they conceive to be a higher place in the scale of society, by means of a larger establishment, horses, carriages, a luxurious table, and a magnificent appropriation of every animal gratification; and in the midst of the most lavish expenditure, Acquisitiveness is in full activity, heaping up luxuries round about the center, self.

People live to get rich, instead of getting rich to live, in the higher acceptation of that term. Love, truth, and beauty, music and poetry, nature and art, these are the true objects of existence; but these are sacrificed, and the greater part of life spent in acquiring riches, merely that we may eat, drink, sleep, clothe, and ride luxuriously, and otherwise lead the life of a mere animal. To be a man in all that distinguishes man from the brute, is not the object, but to get rich; for in the present state of society a man is not measured by his manhood, but by his money. Money secures for us the necessaries of life, leisure, and opportunity for the pursuit of truth and knowledge, the enjoyment and cultivation of the beautiful in nature, art, and above all, it adds to our power of helping others, and makes social intercourse easy and agreeable. For all these purposes money is really power, and its acquisition a legitimate object of pursuit; but when we give the best years of our life to its attainment, after these wants have been reasonably provided for, even worldly aggrandizement is but a poor exchange for our souls. This is the true worship of the devil Mammon, in opposition to the worship of God. We live in this contaminated moral atmosphere, and it is difficult to prevent young people from catching the contagion; but they should be early taught the real objects of life, that they may not lose its end in acquiring the means; that it is within ourselves that the springs of happiness must arise, and not in any external advantages; and that all the highest requirements of our nature God has made as plentiful as pure air and water; and that the power to take in the "landscape" is better even than the possession of the "land" itself. Teach them first " to seek the kingdom of God and His righteousness," with the perfect certainty that all *these things* "shall be added unto them;"—that riches, whether acquired by themselves or others, are a charge and responsibility, to be spent in furthering the development of mind, and the spirit of love in man, and in promoting the happiness of the whole sensitive creation.

In early life the feeling is disposed, particularly when fully developed, to act separately, and a child should be taught to set no value upon anything except in proportion to its utility. The two ideas—the thing, and its use, should never be disjoined. The disposition to hoard, to collect a number of things together for the mere sake of being possessed of them, of callimg them "mine," as much as possible should in every instance be repressed, and they should be valued as the means of giving pleasure to others. What more common ground of nursery strife than the love of possession? The child tired of its plaything, throws it carelessly aside, until his little brother takes it up; the feeling of property rises—he instantly snatches at it, and cries, "Johnnie sha'n't have it! It is *mine!* Papa gave it to *me!*" Johnnie thinks present possession a good title, and holds it fast. A struggle, and perhaps a fight ensues, until nurse settles the question between justice and benevolence as she best can, with very confused notions on the subject—most likely by an angry shake, or box on the ear, of the elder combatant.

It is not intended that children should not be taught to respect others' rights, but merely that they should learn gracefully to yield their own on fitting occasions, when the greater pleasure of others can be gained by it.

Many well-intentioned persons in whom the propensity to acquire is strong, from its having been in constant exercise all their lives, foster selfishness and avarice in their children, while they think only that they are engendering a proper spirit of economy. Many wise saws are employed for this purpose, such as, "a penny saved is a penny gained," etc. There was one mother who told her children always to keep their eyes on the ground when they took a walk, because they possibly might find something that other people had dropped.*

---

*The morbid love of gain is induced by training, and by the prevalent spirit of the household. It is also inherited by the children of parents who crave wealth and make it the prominent thought of daily life. We could fill hundreds of pages with cases illustrating this unnatural development. We give one. A wealthy and thriving merchant has an only son aged twelve years, whose mother recently brought him for a phrenological examination. We found him a bright, intellectual boy, with good moral and social qualities, but he had enormous Acquisitiveness and Secretiveness; and after calling the mother's attention to the abnormal tendency to acquire, and lay up anything and everything, even articles of only imaginary value, she said he already had a bureau full of strings, empty spools, bits of glass, corks, bottles, broken dishes, anything; he also had a box in the wood-house, which would hold a bushel, filled with bits of iron, old broken stove covers, rusty hoops, scrap iron of any sort which he had collected, bit by bit, from the streets, gutters, or vacant lots, all of which he husbanded with a miser's care. To make the matter intense, the boy then took up the story and said, lifting up his coat behind, "You see, sir, this big iron spike which I picked up on the railroad in the country recently, and mamma won't let me carry it in my pocket, so I suspend it by a string around my neck and

If we blame the selfish hoarding of that which might be made most beneficial to others, the waste of it is still more reprehensible; the needless waste of one particle that would be serviceable to others, is wrong. The frugality which avoids this is so distinct in its nature from meanness or stinginess, that it may safely be insisted on with children without fear of making them miserly.

As the abuse of Secretiveness leads to lying, so the abuse of this faculty leads to theft; but both feelings must be badly trained indeed ever to lead to these low and disreputable vices, except in the very necessitous classes. Avarice and covetousness also arise from the undue activity of Acquisitiveness. But we suspect that other abuses of this feeling will be found besides these which lie so evidently upon the surface. If a man consumes more than he produces, it certainly must be at some other's expense; and it is time we began to inquire seriously at whose expense it is.

CONSTRUCTIVENESS.

As the last faculty described gives the desire to acquire and accumulate, so this gives the desire to con-

let it hang down my back under my coat." And sure enough, there it hung, rough and rusty, between his shoulder-blades. When asked if it was not a nuisance, especially when he leaned back in his chair, he replied, "Oh, yes, it is something of a bother, but the pleasure I feel in knowing that I have it, more than makes up for all the annoyance."

The boy had large Benevolence and was very liberal where generous service and not money was called for.

struct, to make machines, and to use tools to enable us to do so. At first sight it may seem to have little to do with moral education, but if employment be necessary to the health of both body and mind, it is very desirable to cultivate that power which disposes us to seek it.

In some children its development is so remarkable that it can not remain unnoticed. Their little fingers are always trying to execute the designs shadowed forth in their imaginations, and though the fair image is apt to look very clumsy and ill-proportioned when it is embodied, the young operatives acquire manual dexterity in their repeated attempts to accomplish their ideas, until the well-rigged boat, the freely-working steam-engine, stand forth in miniature perfection to reward their perseverance. In such cases the faculty will, unless checked by peculiar obstacles, or intellectual deficiencies, go on developing itself until it leads to success in some branch of science or the arts which requires mechanical skill. It might seem necessary to point out the absurdity of compelling such children to enter into a line of profession quite at variance with this natural taste, if we did not so often see it committed. In few children is the faculty so deficient that they might not always employ themselves profitably in its cultivation if materials were afforded them, and if the usual prohibition were not laid upon "making a litter."

Persons who teach music, the piano for instance, know how desirable it is that their pupils should begin early to use the keys, as their fingers then acquire a facility which can not be attained in after-life; in the

THOMAS A. EDISON.
CONSTRUCTIVENESS.

PLATE VII.

same manner children, under the instinctive impulses of this faculty, if properly assisted and instructed, gain a mechanical dexterity of infinite service to them in almost all the pursuits of life, and which might very much lessen the necessary term of apprenticeship to any manual employment. When this facility in the use of the fingers is not acquired early, and when the natural disposition to it is deficient, it can seldom be afterward attained, and an inaptitude for all manual operations will be conspicuous through life. Building houses, bridges, etc., with wooden bricks, or with cards, joining dissected maps, cutting figures on paper, drawing, are all exercises of this faculty, and therefore useful indoor amusements; but it should be borne in mind that children are always happier when a pleasant employment to themselves is also of use to their elders, and they will work with great alacrity at it if their attention be not confined too long. As boys grow older, the juvenile workshop will become an excellent school for the faculty.

In all ranks, power and skill in the use of the hands are most desirable. Vacant minutes and hours may then be filled up with useful and agreeable occupation which would otherwise be devoted to listlessness and *ennui*, and the mind is refreshed for renewed exertion. When the mind has been over-excited or disturbed, manual occupation tranquillizes it, and restores its equilibrium, when study would only increase the evil. In the tedium of sickness its assistance is invaluable, by gently drawing off the attention from the languid and uneasy bodily feelings which accompany the lighter degrees of suffering.

3*

The needle and its kindred labors are the never-failing resource of one sex; and where the faculty of Constructiveness has been properly educated, the pencil, the tool-box, the chemical apparatus, and many other implements of art or science, will furnish the other sex with useful and interesting employment in the intervals of more important avocations, or of mental labors.

When the organ of this faculty is largely developed, it generally leads to great facility in using the fingers for all mechanical purposes; but it is a feeling or sentiment, not an intellectual faculty. It requires to be joined to large Form, Size, Weight, and Imitation, to make a good workman.*

---

* When we consider how many of the comforts of daily life come to us through the use of this faculty, which, joined in action with Causality, constitute the power of invention, we recognize its great, its indispensable necessity to civilization. If the faculty could be blotted out it would remand the human race to a condition of shelterless wandering, thereby making man worse off, in fact, than most of the animal tribes, who are by nature clad in feathers or fur. We have heard respectable people, who are sensible and considerate in most matters, speak contemptuously of mechanism and mechanics, and we have been wicked enough to wish they could be compelled to try life for a while with no aid from the head and hand of the skilled mechanic. If they were brought to the necessity of constructing tools to work with in manufacturing clothing, and shelter, and also implements for tilling the soil and procuring food, they would soon be ashamed of their derision of mechanism and mechanics. Indeed the farmer who raises food, and raw material for ten thousand other articles of comfort and elegance, must use Constructiveness in no small degree. One does not need to build an

CAUTIOUSNESS.

Combativeness gives the desire to meet and to repel danger—Cautiousness, on the contrary, to avoid it. Here is one of Nature's frequent paradoxes; but the result of the two feelings, equally strong, would be judicious courage, prudent energy, and calm circumspection.

A disposition in which this quality is superabundant, will present some of the same difficulties in its management as those proceeding from a secretive temper. A dread of the consequences of speaking the truth may have the same effects as a disposition to hide it. When these original tendencies are found united, it will require a strong exercise of the superior powers of the mind for the maintenance of truth and sincerity on all occasions. Without, however, any disposition to deceit, we sometimes see children of a naturally timid spirit guilty of falsehood under the strong dominion of fear. It does not follow necessarily that the character will prove false; for with the cultivation of the moral powers, moral courage will grow, until falsehood will be feared more than truth, though coupled with any consequences.

The constant and earnest effort of the instructor must be to inspire the moral courage which shall dare to act uprightly, whatever may be the immediate con-

---

engine, a loom, a piano, or a cathedral, to be mechanical. There is scarcely a profession or other pursuit, in which mechanical skill, in some degree, does not become a convenient, if not necessary, factor. All should know how to use tools in some useful work and become theoretically cultured in this faculty as a means of judging of the products we have occasion to deal in or use.

sequences; and also to put the prudence and circumspection which result from a cautious disposition under the guidance of Benevolence, so that they may lead to watchful care and consideration for the interests and well-being of others, rather than to an over-anxiety for those of self.

If the natural development of Cautiousness be too small, children must be taught early to calculate the consequences of actions, and be led to discern the mischiefs which may arise from hasty, ill-advised conduct, in order to guard against rashness and precipitation. How much pain and trouble often originate in one inconsiderate step, a few incautious words!

Cautiousness must be also considered in the relation it bears to physical as well as to moral excitements.

Before children understand the nature of the objects around them they have reason to be cautious, and therefore in them the feeling usually predominates. Education must step in to prevent Caution from degenerating into timidity, and its deficiency from giving rise to heedlessness. If a child be heedless, the most effectual method of cure, when it can be adopted without serious mischief ensuing, is to let him feel fully the consequences of his rashness. If he will put his hand too near the fire, let him be burned; if he will overbalance himself, let him fall; if he will tease the cat, let her scratch him; and these self-taught lessons will make a more lasting impression than many a prudent warning or angry admonition. On the other hand, children who are naturally timid are frequently made cowards by the injudicious care and attention of those around. For example, the child, in attempting to run

D. H. PINGREY.
CAUTIOUSNESS.

PLATE VIII.

alone, tumbles and falls; the whole family start up alarmed; anxious inquiries and ejaculations are poured into the child's ears, until he begins to find out, what he would scarcely have known otherwise, that he has been hurt. Then begins a roar, and then are redoubled the expressions of commiseration, and meanwhile the child thinks to himself, "What a perilous adventure! What a little hero I was to tumble down!" A thousand unheeded bruises would do him less harm than the ill-timed sympathy. From having every trifling mishap made a matter of such prodigious importance, he will soon learn to consider pain a mighty evil, and his own pain especially to be dreaded and guarded against, and will perhaps grow up one of those selfish, calculating persons, who never can persuade themselves to do a good action, without being first morally certain that not the slightest inconvenience will be thereby entailed upon themselves. We do not mean to say that children are to be treated with unkindness and neglect; but it is truer kindness to try to render the mind superior to pains and trials, than to let such pains and trials get the mastery.*

We may hope that the time is almost gone by when

---

* Petting and pitying children when anything of minor consequence occurs to them is very bad policy, for both parent and child. A neighbor of ours had a little girl two or three years old. Whenever she fell while walking she would lie and cry until one of the family ran and picked her up and made an ado over the mishap. Their usage had trained her to expect this. One day she was visiting with our children, and, in running, fell. She started, as usual, to cry, but looking around, remembered that her mother and sister were not there to pity and commiser-

the fears of children are purposely excited by imaginary objects of terror, when superstition is engendered for life in order to enforce temporary obedience; the folly, the cruelty, the wickedness of this practice has become sufficiently obvious to the intelligent, and even nurse-maids have begun to catch the enlightenment of the day in this respect; but there is still another fear which is sometimes too much impressed upon the minds of children, and this is—the fear of death. The representations of death itself in pictures, and in pictures, too, that are given to children for their amusement, are of a hideous and revolting kind. The accompanying circumstances of death, churchyards, sepulchres, and coffins, are associated in their minds with dreariness, gloom, and superstitious horrors. "A child came running into its mother's room one day, sobbing violently, 'Mamma, mamma, I don't like to die; all the dirt will get into my eyes!' and thus it is we spoil the wise arrangements of Providence! introducing them to the childish mind before it can take any but the most partial possible view of them. The child will probably never lose the impression which he that day received from his maid; perhaps will never feel the charm which there is in the thought of that gentle sleep which dissolves our mortal body, and perhaps reposes the spirit, intervening between its earthly and heavenly career." *

There is more to be feared from excessive timidity

---

ate, and she stopped crying, got up and went on with the play, and thus the whole afternoon, she fell a dozen times, but picked herself up and did not cry at all.

* Monthly Repository.

than from too great rashness; we should, therefore, be careful to give this faculty as little stimulation, as little exercise as possible—for every faculty is strengthened by exercise, and weakened by inactivity. Children can no more help feeling afraid than they can help feeling the toothache. It is absurd, therefore, and very injudicious to laugh at their fears, unless a cheerful laugh will help to dispel them and restore confidence. We ought to protect children as much as possible from imaginary fears until they are of an age to see their groundlessness and until other feelings have acquired sufficient strength to supply moral courage. Feelings are aroused more by sympathy with others than by precept and lectures; particularly is fear caught from what is seen of the feeling manifested by those about us. Richter says, "One scream of fear from a mother may resound through the whole life of her daughter; for no rational discourse can extinguish the mother's scream."* Early fears have nothing to do with reason, and are to be treated as we would treat a bodily ailment. However unreasonable their fears, do not force children to bear them; show their groundlessness, if possible, and accustom them to objects of terror by degrees. Never let us judge of their state of mind by our own. We say this equally with reference to all the feelings, for in no case are the feelings of a child and of a grown-up person alike. This too common mistake of judging children by ourselves is productive of infinite error and wrong. Timidity, over-caution, indecision, arise from the excess of Cautiousness, and such weaknesses are

---

* Levana, or The Doctrine of Education.

incompatible with greatness, or even with success in any high object.*

Large Cautiousness and small Combativeness lead to excessive timidity; that is, to natural cowardice.

Very large Cautiousness and small Hope produce great depression and despondency, and a gloomy view of all things, frequently leading to suicide.

Combativeness, Destructiveness, and Cautiousness in excess, make an irritable, peevish temper.

LOVE OF LIFE.

This faculty produces an instinctive wish to preserve life for its own sake, independently of the pleasure or pain with which it may be accompanied. It induces men to cling to life in circumstances in which other-

---

* Natural timidity, through excessive Cautiousness, may co-exist in a child with large Combativeness, which, when aroused, produces force and courage; and in character they act alternately, or in harmony, according to the nature and influence of circumstances. The little boy who was afraid to go to bed in an adjoining room, on account of the darkness, and because he sometimes heard rats running in the walls and ceiling, was cured by having a long stick placed in his hands by his father, with directions to whip on the wall when he heard the rats running. He waited to hear their noise, and when it was begun, he whipped on the wall and silenced them. He had won a victory. The exercise of Combativeness gave him pleasure; his Cautiousness was silenced; and every night he was in a hurry to have darkness and bedtime come so that he might watch for the rats, stick in hand.

JACOB M. HOWARD.

VITATIVENESS—LOVE OF LIFE.

PLATE IX.

wise existence might not be thought desirable. This instinctive feeling it is which, perhaps, more than reason or principle, prevents men escaping from temporary suffering by suicide. It is this feeling, assisted by Hope and Wonder (Spirituality), which has, in all countries, unaided by a supernatural revelation, originated the idea of a future state. Little can be said here with reference to the education of the feeling, although much mischief results from the too common mode of treating the subject of death. The consequence of the injudicious representations so frequently made is the great dread of death that sometimes embitters the whole of life; the only antidote to which feeling is the faith which enables us to place our ultimate fate, with unbounded confidence, in the hands of our Father who is in Heaven.*

---

*While making phrenological examinations at an Asylum for the Insane, a party of ladies was collected for the purpose. I supposed the persons to be attendants or nurses. Of the third subject I remarked, "You have an excellent constitution, and ought, with proper care, to live until you are ninety. Besides, you have such excessive LOVE OF LIFE that you will hold on until the last drop of vitality shall be exhausted;" and turning to the matron, remarked, "If this woman ever becomes insane it will be through fear of death, arising from the morbid activity of that faculty." The matron replied, "She is a patient, and that is her point of difficulty. She gets an idea that she is going to die and thinks no man can prevent her death but the Medical Superintendent of the Institution."

The patient thus learned, intellectually, what the trouble was, and resolved to rise above it. Her husband visited her the next day, and she told him she was organized to live to be ninety, that her expectation and fear of death was

THE SELF-REGARDING FEELINGS.
SELF-ESTEEM.

Self-esteem must not be confounded with *selfishness*, which belongs to all the lower feelings of our nature; although when naturally powerful, or when undisciplined by the superior faculties, it fearfully increases the activity of the lower feelings. Self-respect or esteem of ourselves, when associated, as it ought to be, with the moral sentiments, is a powerful instrument of good. It is absolutely essential to decision of character, and to the maintenance of a straightforward course in the path of rectitude; for, as we can have no reliance upon ourselves without it, no faith in our own judgment, we shall be continually liable to swerve on one side or the other under the influences of opposing opinions. It is better, perhaps, on the whole, to have too much rather than too little of the feeling. Of those who have put themselves prominently forward in the world, either for good or for evil, few have been deficient in it. The fear of self-degradation is a powerful aid in the resistance against temptation. Honor, which is in most cases another name for Self-esteem, when properly founded, can not allow its possessor to descend to meanness, to improper pursuits or companions, and it will do much to prevent the debasing indulgence of the inferior propensities.*

---

due not to fact, but to her mental development, and she was going to leave the institution and go home with him. And she did go home, that day, and she has not been back, though years have passed.

*In the United States we have really a deficiency of Self-esteem. We live too little in the atmosphere of per-

J. F. G. MITTAG, M.D.

SELF-ESTEEM.

PLATE X.

Richter says: "Do not fear the rise of the sentiment of honor, which is nothing worse than the rough husk of Self-esteem, or the expanded cover of the tender wings which elevate above the earth, and its flowers. But to raise and ennoble that honor of the individual into honor of the race, and that again into honor of the worth of mind, never praise him who has gained a prize, but those who rank below him; give the honorable title, not as a distinction for the steps which have been mounted, but as a notification of neighborhood to what is higher; and lastly, let your praise afford more pleasure because it shows that you are pleased than for the distinction it gives."

---

sonal independence, and too much in that of vanity, ambition, and the applause of men. We think people are proud, when they are only vain, fond of dress, show, and extravagant display. Self-esteem does not boast, dress, or act for the eyes and approval of others. It proudly stands erect, does duty as dictated by reason and conscience or necessity, exercises economy if liberal expenditure can not be indulged in, dresses plainly if necessary, and lives in small houses if no better can be afforded, and frankly says, "I would like better things and a higher style of living, but I can not afford them." When we have more Self-esteem we shall build fewer mansions and more cottages—there will be fewer decorations in houses, furniture, and equipage, and also fewer mortgages, less pretense, and more solid worth and happiness. Men may properly console themselves with pride in a long line of honorable ancestors, and wisely resolve not to break the chain which should link the past with the future, and when tempted in any way to belittle their character and do dishonorable things, may properly say with one of old, "Is thy servant a dog that he should do this thing?"

And what is a proper foundation for self-respect? The consciousness that our feelings and conduct obey, in the main, the dictates of duty and benevolence, and that these latter reign too powerfully in our minds to permit any unworthy passion to acquire dominion over us; in fact, to feel assured that the man predominates in us, and not the mere animal. If, instead of this ground for self-respect, we value ourselves upon possessions, external advantages, or accomplishments, upon anything whatever which appeals to our inferior nature, Self-esteem will degenerate into self-importance and pride.

In children we continually see the faculty called into exercise by objects that should never be allowed to excite it; they are noticed for being "nicely dressed," or for their good looks; for their activity and cleverness in some particular way; for being able to recite fluently a number of words with which their memory has been loaded without much thought of their meaning; and for numberless things which have no excellence in themselves, but which produce an abundant crop of conceit.

We have sometimes thought that at a very early age, the feeling of self-importance is unduly excited in children, even under the most enlightened management. The solicitude which they observe in all around them for their comfort and enjoyment, the watchful care which even anticipates their wants and wishes, the immediate sympathy which all their feelings receive, conspire to give them ideas of their own importance destined to be cruelly upset when the attractions of infancy are over; if, indeed, these ideas do not produce a lasting impression on the character.

If a child has naturally a large share of the disposition under consideration, reproof, unless very judiciously administered, and still more contempt or ridicule, will be apt to increase rather than to subdue it. Instead of inducing humility, they will urge on the feeling to its perversion—self-sufficiency, and create, perhaps, a moroseness and closeness of feeling, which beyond anything else shuts up the mind from happiness and improvement.

When the feeling is in excess, there will be a constant use of "I," and "Myself." Everything will center in or move around this "I, myself," and everything will be regarded only as it has reference to this important first person singular. Such children will constantly require to be kept back. The charm of modesty will always be wanting in their character. They will open a conversation with strangers on terms of perfect equality, like a young acquaintance of ours, whose comments upon his mother's method in the education of his younger brothers and sisters show how far more capable of the task he conceives himself to be. In early management, it will be better not to notice this self-worship and self-exaltation; to be careful not to repeat the child's sayings and doings, and, above all things, to endeavor to excite an interest *in things themselves for their own sake*. Interest children all day long in their studies, pleasures, and pursuits, and give them no time to think of themselves. Of course we do not mean by this, to exclude self-knowledge, of all knowledge the most desirable in such a case. If children are made to feel how all that we possess of real beauty and excellence, whether in body or mind, is the gift of

God, without any merit on our part—how much more of excellence and beauty we might possess, had we used due diligence—how great are our faults and deficiencies, compared with that excellence of which we can conceive—it is almost sure to engender humility, and prevent them from thinking "more highly of themselves than they ought to think."

The feeling may be too weak, and then it leads to irresolution and indecision, to the want of manliness and independence of character, to over-submissiveness and the desire to lean on others—under these circumstances it must be stimulated.

The abuses of this feeling, in excess, are very numerous. In childhood it gives rise to pettishness and willfulness, to impatience of control, and rebellion against authority, and to an extreme sensitiveness and readiness to take offense. Later in life, it produces pride, arrogance, conceit, love of power, dogmatism, insolence, tyranny; everything is overrated connected with self; in common language, "the geese are all swans."

There are many checks to this feeling in excess. Children may be taught how Self-esteem, in proportion to its natural strength, always colors the self-estimate they make of all their actions and possessions; how all they are and all they have are derived, and their thankfulness and pride should be directed to the true source from whence they are derived; and above all, they should be taught never to pride themselves on what they possess, but if at all on the manner in which they make use of their possessions.

LOVE OF APPROBATION.
(APPROBATIVENESS).

The desire of standing well in the estimation of others, is one of the most powerful motives to human action, and as public opinion generally takes the side of virtue, is a strong check upon the predominance of the selfish passions in society; nevertheless, being as it is but a selfish and inferior motive, it must be carefully confined within its proper bounds, and the feeling will then only induce so much regard for the approval of others, as is consistent with the dictates of the moral sense. So guarded, it becomes the source of one of our purest pleasures—the sympathy and approbation of the wise and good.

Under proper culture, children in early infancy will look to the approbation of their parents as their chief reward, and to their disapprobation as their chief punishment. The sentiment is, therefore, one of high importance in the first stage of existence, and the more it is exercised in that direction, to the exclusion of all other rewards and penalties, the better. But as the intellectual and moral powers grow in strength, its importance will proportionately decrease, until it attains its just rank among the other instincts. This craving for admiration is, however, so rarely managed judiciously in childhood, that we seldom see it in mature years subservient to the higher powers. When other feelings have arrived at sufficient strength and maturity, it would be as well to drop the appeal to this altogether. Let the motive be love, or respect, or conscience, or kindness; not praise. Praise, which is the expression of the approval of others, is continually substituted as the incentive to good conduct, for those higher motives to which we have before alluded—the satisfaction which results from having done right, and of having assisted to make others happy. "Let Miss Such-an-one hear how well you can say pretty prayers," is a case in point. The lesson sometimes takes a worse form. "Do so and so, my darling, and then mamma will love you better than brother Harry." It would be well if the pleasure of parents in good conduct took oftener the character of sympathy than of approbation, that the expression should not be so much in the form, "You have been good to-day, and mamma loves you for it," as, "Because mamma loves you, she is glad *with you* that you have been good to-day."

It is not intended that praise should not accompany right conduct, but that the pleasure thus excited should be kept subordinate to the higher one. When the higher one appears to be a sufficient motive, a wise parent will be careful how he add a lower one, lest it should be the means of weakening instead of strengthening the power of the former. He will make his child understand, that the world frequently condemns what is right and approves what is wrong, and, therefore, to enable himself to persevere in the path of duty, he must learn to feel the consciousness of self-approval a sufficient reward. Self-respect is necessary to this end, and with such a view the feeling which excites it must be cultivated, if it appear to be naturally deficient.

Richter says, " The desire to please with some good quality which rules only in the visible or external king-

LEON GAMBETTA.
APPROBATIVENESS.
PLATE XI.

dom, is so innocent and right, that the opposite, to be indifferent, or disagreeable, to the eye or ear, would even be wrong. Why should a painter dress to please the eye, and not his wife? I grant you there is a poisonous vanity and love of approbation; that, namely, which lowers the inner kingdom to an outer one, spreads out sentiments as snaring nets for the eye and ear, and degradingly buys and sells itself with that which has real inherent value. Let a girl try to please with her appearance, and her dress, but never with holy sentiments; a so-called fair devotee, who knew that she was so, would worship nothing save herself, the devil, and her admirer. Every mother, and every friend of the family, should keep a careful watch over their own wish to praise—often as dangerous as that to blame—which so easily names and praises an unconscious grace in the expressions of the affections, in the mien, or in the sentiments, and thereby converts it forever into a conscious one; that is to say, kills it."

In some children, little girls especially, this appetite for admiration is so keen and insatiable, that not a word, look, or action escapes untinctured by some covert design upon the admiration of bystanders, and childhood loses entirely its two greatest charms, simplicity and impulsiveness. It is most unfortunate when a mother is unconscious of the strength of this propensity in her child, and deceives herself by mistaking the goodness on the surface for real excellence, and fosters the weakness every minute by indiscriminating praise. Two children may be seen, the one with large love of approbation, the other with small. The latter will sit complacently eating her sweetmeats without offering any to her companions, nothing disturbed by their longings and the half injunctions of the elder bystanders to be a good, generous child, and give some away. The other child, with perhaps an equal love of eating, will eagerly and somewhat ostentatiously share all with her playfellows. The difference in the degree of virtue in the two children is not so great that one should be reproached as a little selfish glutton, and the other extolled as a pattern of generosity; the difference is simply, that the one likes sugar-plums better than praise, and the other likes praise better than sugar-plums. Nevertheless, in nine cases out of ten, the disposition of the latter is very much to be preferred, since the desire for approbation is a much higher feeling than the mere animal pleasure of eating; and a generous action, done even from an imperfect motive, renders a person more fit for the reception of better influences. The greedy child is hardened more and more after every act of greediness, and still more if it is scolded and made to dislike its companions by being placed in odious comparison with them; but a sunshine will be reflected upon the little giver from the happy, grateful faces of the other children, which would be quite sufficient reward, if not overlaid and extinguished by an eulogium.

Commendation in words is more likely to foster vanity than a kiss or look of affection. Comparisons with other children should be carefully avoided, and all that induces self-consciousness. For this reason, tales for their entertainment should be more about good children, that is, children who are naturally good without any parade, than about good and bad children.

Let us now speak of this faculty in its abuse. The love of dress exists in the present age in great excess, but let us be careful not to run into an opposite extreme. Beauty of body is desirable as well as excellence of mind, and in checking too great a display of personal vanity in our daughter, we must not on the contrary inflict upon society an ill-dressed, ungraceful, slatternly eccentric, who values only mental superiority, to the entire neglect of the equally legitimate mode of pleasing by the person. Richter says: " While man finds a cothurnus (buskin), on which to raise and show himself to the world in the judge's seat, literary rank, the professor's chair, or the car of victory, woman has nothing save her outward appearance whereon to raise and display her inner nature; why pull from under her this lowly footstool of Venus? . . . . We will now pass to the clothes-devil, as the old theologians formerly called the toilet. . . . . The preachers do not sufficiently bear in mind, that to a woman her dress is the third organ of the soul (the body is the second and the brain the first), and every upper garment one organ more. . . . . Woman's love of dress has, along with cleanliness, which dwells on the very borders between physical nature and morality, a next-door neighbor in purity of heart. Why are all girls who go out to meet princes with addresses and flowers, dressed in white? The chief color of the mentally and physically pure English woman is white. Hess found white banners used most in free countries; and I find States all the more modest the freer they are. I will become no surety for the inner purity of a woman who only puts on the color of purity when walking in the streets." . . . . With reference to the over-love of dress, he says: "Animate the heart, and it no longer thirsts for common air, but for ether. No one is less vain than a bride. . . . . Ascribe to cleanliness, symmetry, propriety of dress, and all the æsthetic requisites of beauty, their brilliant and true worth; so a daughter, like a poet, forgets herself in her art and in her ideal, and her own beauty in what is beautiful." . . . . Finally, he says: "Woman's body is the pearl oyster; whether this be brilliant and many-colored, or rough and dark from the place of its birth, yet the pure white pearl within alone gives it value. I mean by this thy heart, thou good maiden—thou who expectest not to be appreciated, but only to be misunderstood!"

The ordinary modes of school-education tend to foster the excess of this emotion. To stand above his school-fellows is too much the object of the school-boy's ambition, and he is naturally tempted to rejoice at their want of success which keeps them below him, rather than in their advance together with himself. The meanness and unworthy passions which often enter into the contest for a prize, are faithful types of those which the world displays on a larger scale. Envy and jealousy spring out of the love of approbation in excess, when uncontrolled by superior feelings, and all methods of education which tend to excite them are to be condemned.

Zschokke says: "It is treason to the holy nature of childhood to address ourselves in the management of children rather to the covetousness of sordid self-interest, than to the innate consciousness of the true and the noble. The charlatanry of public school examinations was banished from my seminary. They may sometimes prove the merits of the teachers, but never those of the pupils."

Childish vanity, another of the signs of this excess, should never be treated as a crime; in some instances it might be advisable to let a child learn by experience the paltriness of the enjoyment arising from its gratification. For example:* "C. was very vain of some jewels, the gift of an injudicious relative; or as she emphatically called them, her *do-ills*. Day after day she asked to wear them. Day after day her mother said 'No,' but finding that to refuse was of no use, she was puzzled what course to adopt, until it occurred to her to let one fire put another out. Accordingly the next time C. applied to her for permission to wear her *do-ills*, she answered: 'Certainly, wear them if you please; but you know these things are valuable because your mamma's dear friend gave them to you; they must neither be lost nor spoiled. If you have them on, you must remain in this room, and even I think I should say, upon this chair, in order to be sure they are safe.' C. consented to the terms, and joyfully bedecked herself with her finery, and then stationed herself upon a chair. It was a fine evening in August, and the other children were out; however, for two hours C. persevered in sitting on the chair. At length she begged to have them taken off, and from that time to this (two years) the *do-ills* have never been mentioned but with an uncomfortable feeling and a blush. The plan here adopted answered very well to check

---

* Monthly Repository.

vanity in that direction; but against vanity about dress and all other things, there is but one real remedy, the substitution of love of excellence for the love of excelling; the development of the intellect also will bring about a just appreciation of the value of dress, etc., when weighed against mental superiority.'"*

Bashfulness arises from an excess of the Love of Approbation, and modesty is ordinarily connected with a moderate Self-esteem, but it has been well observed: " Bashfulness and modesty, although so frequently confounded, have yet no necessary connection or relationship, and either may exist without the presence of the other. The former, or shamefacedness, as it is often called, is a weakness not unfrequently belonging to the physical constitution, and of which every one would gladly be relieved. It may be a quality of those even who are most impure in their feelings, and when unrestrained, most immodest in their conversation. Modesty, on the other hand, pertains especially to the mind, is the subject of education, and the brightest, and I had almost said, the rarest gem that adorns the human character. That awkward diffidence, so frequently met with in the young of both sexes, is of a nature, too often, very little akin to modesty."

However useful the desire of estimation, the love of applause, fame, or glory may be, yet it must be admitted that the feeling from which these legitimate uses spring is far too strong in the present day; for it is this feeling which gives to public opinion and to fashion their power. How much is done from the fear of the folk, and of what Mrs. Grundy will say, instead of from

---

* Monthly Repository.

the fear of God, or of doing wrong; and who dares to be unfashionable, although following fashion may cost him all real good! Much, if not most, of what we regard as virtue in the world, is merely the tribute which vice pays to virtue—it is merely the seeming which this faculty puts on in deference to society, and to gain the name and wages of virtue without its reality; it is not real gold, only counterfeit. This feeling is essentially selfish in its nature, and its characteristic is to love distinction, not the excellence by which alone distinction ought to be acquired; it is satisfied with appearing to be, without being. And herein is the difference between the higher sentiments and this: that these *act*, the other only *talks ;* and yet it is very difficult for most people to distinguish between the counterfeit virtue and the real—to distinguish between what is done for applause and out of deference to the opinion of the society in which we live, and what is done from a real sense of rectitude. People are even very apt to deceive *themselves* in this particular. They have all their lives been wearing the clothes of virtue, and talking virtuously, and seeming virtuous, and even doing many virtuous acts; and they wonder at the end of their lives that they are esteemed so lightly. But let such persons examine themselves carefully and honestly, as to whether there has not been more seeming than doing, and whether they have not taken care to get paid in applause for even what they have done. Society, in consequence, instinctively feels that it owes them nothing. They have blown their own trumpet before them—they have let their right hand know what their left has done, and they have had their reward.

That too many work for thanks and gratitude, and

not from real benevolence or a sense of duty, is evidenced by the too common saying, "What is the use of helping such people, you get no thanks for your pains," or "What is the use of attempting to do good, you meet with nothing but ingratitude for your trouble," etc.; whereas, had they been virtuous for virtue's sake —from a sense of duty or benevolence—no thanks or gratitude, which is only praise in another shape, would have been expected. The guinea which is extracted from us in our passage between the plates held by two fashionable or titled ladies—do we ever think of it afterward, or watch its application? which we should do, if the good of the cause for which it was given was our object, instead of the payment of a tax to public opinion and the fear of the folk: many subscriptions, and much church-going, emanate from love of approbation alone.

If we do good to be paid in gratitude, we are certain to be disappointed, and we must learn to do good for its own sake, or not at all. The people generally can not raise themselves above their own state of feeling, if it be one in which the selfish feelings habitually predominate. They judge others by themselves, and can scarcely conceive of a really unselfish motive; or if they can, they would regard an action as folly which has no direct bearing on self-interest. The philanthropist, therefore, must expect to have his motives and actions misjudged and misrepresented. If as a clergyman he visits the poor, he must hear it said, he is only doing his duty, he is paid for it, and he wants to get people to go to church because he lives by it, the same as another man lives by his shop and is anxious to get customers. If he would serve the poor through the establishment of public institutions, it is considered that power, and place, and social consideration and position are his motives; and the people have some excuse for this mode of knowing things, for they have been too much courted and flattered for the power and influence which their numerical force often confers, and not from any wish to do real good to themselves. We must learn also to do good for its own sake, because the more we study the cause of the evils inherent in society the more we must become convinced that eleemosynary charity, which alone is popular, and paid in thanks and praise, tends rather to foster and nourish the evil than to cure it. To insist upon the only means which are really efficacious to raise the condition of the poor, viz: providence, prudence, forethought, economy, education, and to help the poor to help themselves, is not the popular course.

There are other minor abuses, such as flattering others, that they may praise us—sacrificing truth and sincerity rather than give offense; but their notice comes more properly under another head. If Conscientiousness be naturally strong and well cultivated, there is no fear of the love of praise leading to insincerity and meanness.

But everywhere the spirit of democracy is on the increase, and all men, whether consciously or not, are aiding it by their exertions; and with this increase, and the penny press, and the greatly increasing facility of communication, and, in fact, with everything that enables man to act more directly upon man, public opinion becomes more powerful and irresistible, and in proportion as it thus becomes more powerful is it lowered to the mental and moral level of the increasing multitude from whence that power is derived. No doubt this is good on the whole, as the world is made for the happiness of all, not of a class; but, nevertheless, it everywhere tends to exalt mediocrity and to make popular that only which is capable of being understood and appreciated, not by the highest minds and intellects, but the lowest. On this account it is that above all things moral training must be directed to enable children to act in perfect independence of the public voice, and carefully to study and to do what is right irrespective of it. In America few have moral courage to breathe a whisper against public opinion, and with the increasing power of the majority in this country (England) we are daily approaching a similar condition of mental slavery. We have also equally to guard against the misrule of fashion; for, as the distinguished author of "Adam Bede" says, "Our moral sense learns the manners of good society, and smiles when others smile."

The study of the mental faculties, and the legitimate objects to which they point, will show us that mankind have set up false gods—that they worship golden calves—that the true end and aim of life is sacrificed to these idols, and that if we can but free ourselves from an undue thralldom to custom and habit and fashion, we may be much happier, and attain all that is worth living for at a much less cost, and at a much less sacrifice. To achieve this emancipation, we must be early taught not to fear the world's dread laugh, more especially when we are in the right; we must be prepared "to stand approved in the sight of God, though worlds judge us perverse."

Let children, then, be early taught to set a true and

just value upon public opinion. A thousand fools can not make *one* wise man, for nought multiplied by nought, even a thousand times, is still nought. Show them how the world has always treated its greatest men —how it has stoned its Prophets, crucified its Saviours, martyred its Apostles. Show how fickle, how indiscriminating it is to this day—how ignorance speaks with the same confidence, or even with more than knowledge—how the heights and depths of the greatest minds are measured at once by the conceit of the smallest. Show how hard it is for people to praise, how easy to blame; for many think they show their sense by being able to find fault, but it requires a much higher sense to find out and appreciate excellencies. Call the attention of the young to the kind of criticisms thus current of both men and things in this much dreaded society, and let them say, if they really seek excellence, whether they ought to value such criticism. It requires great talent and long study to master any one subject; but when they have done so, let them listen to the flippant, trivial, conceited, shallow judgments of their acquaintance upon it, and let them learn from that to appreciate the worth of public opinion, and judge whether the desire of fame, based upon such a public opinion, is worth striving for, or ought much to influence their motives to action. To appreciate a great man, requires, if not one as great, still a great man, and the judgments of the world therefore must be either borrowed or erroneous—more frequently the latter, as self-conceit usually supplies any deficiency of talent;

" Whatever Nature has in worth denied,
　She gives in large recruits of needful pride."

Upon whom does Fame bestow her rewards? Really upon those who most deserve them. Does conscience approve the judgment even of the most intimate friends with respect to our characters; how then can we expect the world, or posterity, to do justice; and who would value praise or blame that is not discriminating and just? The originators of useful reforms are generally persecuted, for they get the ill-will of all who lived on the abuses sought to be removed, while those who are benefited usually think the good comes from nature. They who really work, and in the modest quiet of their studies gradually prepare the world for new truths, are unnoticed and neglected; but he who becomes the mouthpiece of this public opinion, when formed—who has brains enough to appreciate, but not to originate, and who can talk—this is the man whom the world pays, and fame immortalizes.

The world scarcely yet recognizes any higher motives than those that arise from Self-esteem and Love of Approbation, that is, the love of power and of fame and glory, which is only another name for applause—the stupid staring and the loud huzzas of the multitude. The hero and the silly coquette are still put upon an equality as to motive; both are in pursuit of fame and glory! Power and fame, as means, are perfectly legitimate and worthy objects of desire, but not as ends; as Tennyson says:

> "Fame with man,
> Being but ampler means to serve mankind,
> Should have small rest or pleasure in herself,
> But work as vassal to the larger love,
> That dwarfs the petty love of one to one."

As ends, as something to rest satisfied with, nothing can be more contemptible. The love of power and of applause are perfectly self-regarding, and whatever fine-sounding names they may take, such as love of fame or glory, must be looked upon with great suspicion as motives to action. The trumpet of fame has hitherto been blown before false heroes, and glory has too often waded through blood and slaughter to the world's destruction and desolation. Yet, a young world, making its gods "after its own image," could conceive no higher motive with which to invest them. They were made jealous of power, greedy and still more jealous of praise, and their *glory* was regarded as the end and aim of creation. Power was worshiped for its own sake, without reference to the end to which it was applied—even though it was generally recognized as swift to damn, slow to save—and praise unceasing and indiscriminating was offered up as the most acceptable service and as the best means of turning this power to individual advantage. Gratitude toward a benefactor is a most noble feeling to be fostered and encouraged; but to praise another, whether God or man, for what can be got by it, is, of all feelings, the meanest. A noise of pots and pans and sounding kettles is used by tribes in Africa to prevent an eclipse, and an equally *senseless* noise of "praise" is used by other tribes to prevent other anticipated disasters, no doubt with the same effect. This abuse of the truly "self-regarding" feelings is most blighting to all our higher aspirations, particularly if it have a religious sanction, and if any portion of such abuse has descended to our own day, the sooner it can be obliterated the better. The abuse of Self-esteem is pride; of Approbativeness, vanity, and in the present little insight that there is into character, they are often mistaken for each other in their mode of manifestation.

Love of Approbation and Benevolence being large give a great disposition to oblige and make it difficult to say "no"; the same joined to good Conscientiousness, moderate Self-esteem, and Secretiveness, produce great openness, truthfulness, and sincerity, and pleasing and obliging manners.*

---

* Nothing is more common than to hear people speak of the action of Approbativeness as the foundation of pride. We can make the distinction between Approbativeness and Self-esteem clear, by the following incident:

A farmer of our acquaintance was about to start for the village to sell a load of potatoes, which he had just been digging. His wife came running to the door and said, "Why, John, I hope you are not going to the village with that old ragged coat on!" "Yes, I am; they *all know me* at the village."

The next day he drove up from the field with another load, which he was going to take for sale to an adjoining town. The wife, with extra anxiety, accosted him. "Now, John, you certainly must not go with that old coat. Wait a minute, and I will bring you a better one." He replied, "*Nobody knows me there.*"

The wife, having larger Approbativeness, wanted her husband to look tidy and respectable when he was going to the village where they went to church, to the stores, public festivals, etc., because they were so well known there—and when he went elsewhere, she desired him to dress well even when in the rough, dirty work of handling and selling potatoes, because the people were wholly or mainly strangers. The husband, on the contrary, with moderate Approbativeness, cared little for a tidy appear-

THE SOCIAL AFFECTIONS.

AMATIVENESS.

This feeling produces love between the sexes. It is not developed in early life, and the period of its development is different in different constitutions. At the time of its coming into activity the moral feelings also acquire greater strength, and become more active; its end is marriage. Before the period at which this feeling is developed, the boy or girl ought to have been instructed in the physiology of both mind and body—in respect to the use and abuse of all their faculties, and with a properly balanced development, there is no fear when all the other feelings have been properly trained, that this one will be abused. The mystery usually made to surround this subject in no way furthers the promotion of true modesty, and ordinarily lets loose upon the mind much misdirected feeling, disturbing its balance, and unsettling its object. They whose experience is intended to guide the young

---

ance while doing dirty work, and having larger Self-esteem, he was independent of a public sentiment which might be supposed to demand good clothes while doing rough work. So he declined to change, because they *all* knew him in one place, and because, in the other place, *none* knew him. His motives and feelings were just the opposite of those of his wife. He manifested pride and independence. She would have worn nice clothes while doing inappropriate work, to please the eyes of both acquaintances and strangers, and perhaps have excited, in both, criticism for her ill-timed and improvident mode of dress. In this she would show her vanity and want of proper independence, while his course showed that he had more pride than vanity.

should recollect that the object of their instruction should be to refine and idealize this propensity, and to associate it always with the higher feelings; for when the feeling is constitutionally strong, it may act irrespective of all but itself. An all-absorbing feeling of love may co-exist with a perfect knowledge that the object of this passion is altogether unworthy of it. Never forget, therefore, "that a man has choice to begin love, but not to end it."

Love, based upon this faculty, becomes a passion and is, undoubtedly, the strongest feeling in our nature. While it exists it absorbs all other feelings, or, at least, is made the center around which all other interests and feelings revolve. It changes the whole nature, frequently giving force and power and brilliancy to the dullest clods of earth. But under its scorching influence, the homely, every-day duties of life are dried up and become tasteless and insipid. It is a temperature in which the common virtues can not exist—they pale and die. Love, as a passion, therefore, is not intended to be a common state of mind, or ever to last long. Probably our first love ought ever to be our last, for its commencement, in all well-regulated minds, being always controllable, it ought to be indulged only when it can lead to matrimony, and the use of so intense a heat of feeling is then to fuse two individual souls into one for life. Having answered this purpose of making two people one for life, the feeling is no longer an all-absorbing passion, but takes its place among the other feelings in due relative proportion to them, first as love, and then as affection. Infinite mischief is done by that class of writers whose works tend

M. SOLER.

AMATIVENESS.

PLATE XII.

to weaken the influence of the marriage tie, representing it as less sacred and less binding by nature than it is by custom; who make a plaything of love, and whose heroes and heroines indulge a succession of little passions, not thinking the affection which remains when passion is dead good enough for such exalted souls, whether the object of that affection be husband, wife, betrothed, or what not. This getting up a passion for one object after another, under the plea of sympathy of soul and intellect, superiority to conventionality, etc., may be a circumstance of much interest and pleasurable excitement in the pages of a novel, and even interwoven with much beauty of thought and sentiment. But in real life such principles are false, dangerous, ruinous. If love has been allowed to expand into passion at a proper time and upon a proper object, and if marriage has resulted, what were two people before, become so thoroughly one, that none of those cross loves take place afterward which form the staple of the works of the writers we have characterized, and are the sole source of their absorbing interest. Marriage, under any circumstances, without love, is opposed to all the laws of our nature, and no writer can paint too strongly the evils which result; but it is only in fiction that these evils are mitigated by casting away the duties which marriage always brings.

As marriage without love is inherently wrong, it can not be made right by the dying injunction of a parent, or from the wish to save a parent from poverty or even ruin. We frequently meet with works of fiction, in which this self-sacrifice is eloquently represented as the highest heroism. But however high-sounding, this is false morality, for supposing that it were right for children to sacrifice themselves for their parents—a young life to an old one, of which we think there is reason to doubt; yet it can not be right to sacrifice those to whom they are married, which they would do by marrying them from any other motive than because they loved them. To do anything that we would not do from the clear dictates of our own reason and conscience, out of deference to the dead or dying, is gross superstition, or at best, it is but the lower feelings of affection mastering the higher.

Marriages are made in heaven, that is, are of the soul's affections; but for the sake of the offspring they require to be publicly registered on earth. Marriage is no longer generally recognized as a religious ceremony, and such registry is now considered by law as sufficient. As it has frequently happened in other observances, the spirit has been lost in the form, and the marriage rite or register is alone thought of in speaking of marriage; whereas the mere form which consults the interests of society, without the union of the affections, is no more a marriage than the taking the teetotal pledge is temperance; and marriage may truly exist, although peculiar circumstances may have made the form *impossible;* but the good of society requires that such marriages should not be formed, for the sake of the general law with which that good is at present so intimately connected.*

---

* No emotion is more influential in character than this, yet in respect to none is there more ignorance and error on the subject of its due regulation and training. Virtue, modesty, and morality, as people have learned to recognize

PHILOPROGENITIVENESS.
(PARENTAL LOVE).

The law of offspring is what this term implies, but in the absence of children, its legitimate object, it is capable of taking a variety of other directions. It is sometimes manifested by children in a remarkable degree. In them it is generally directed toward the lower animals, and there are many good feelings and habits of mind which it excites and encourages.

The child who loves his pet dog, his pet bird, sup-

---

them, have been employed as a barrier against the dissemination of any appropriate knowledge respecting the sexual instinct, and thousands of the best people in the world vainly imagine that ignorance in this direction is the great safeguard of the young. Meantime nature is developing in their constitutions the love element, and it is not in the province of silence or prudery to ignore its power or neutralize its influence. These facts exist, and the true question is, shall this instinct be regulated by an enlightened intellect and sound moral sentiment, or shall it be permitted to revel in ignorance with all the vigor of a blind passion? A large share of the popular literature is calculated to inflame this passion; and such is the perversion of public sentiment that no paper, intended for the million, can become popular and remunerative which is not largely filled with love stories; and three-quarters of the books in Sunday-school libraries are religious stories in which love and marriage are the culmination. Yet the parents of the Sunday-school pupils who read these pious love stories, would sternly repel physiological truth which would enable the young to regard this subject from a scientific point of view, thereby gaining power to regulate their emotions by understanding them. They are thereby left to be the vic-

plies its wants and protects it from danger, he pays attention to its habits and learns how to make it happy. This love for his favorite may, and most likely will, extend itself to the whole sensitive creation. The knowledge he has thus acquired even of one individual, and the habit of tending it, will prevent him from showing cruelty to animals in general; for cruelty more frequently originates in ignorance and thoughtlessness than in natural disposition.

The manifestation of this propensity is not confined to the animate creation—the inanimate claims a share. The little girl loves her doll, she dresses it, puts it care-

---

tims of the torrid, malarial atmosphere of salacious literature, albeit it may be covered with romantic, literary, and even religious gauze. We know that boys who are judiciously and thoroughly instructed by books and oral teaching before this emotion becomes active, may be kept, up to manhood, as pure in spirit and entirely free from vulgar associations of thought, as any good mother could wish her daughter to be. The same boys, if taught by prudish public sentiment to regard esoteric physiological subjects as something to be dreamed of in silence, with only the companionship of vulgar imagination, will become slaves, like others, to the hidden and unregulated fires which tend to consume and debase, instead of broadening and blessing the character. Marriage involves Amativeness, but the life-union of two lovers originates in the faculty of

CONJUGALITY,

recognized and accepted by the leading American phrenologists, though many years ago, spoken of as probable by some Europeans. This organ is located in the cerebrum outward from Philoprogenitiveness, while Amativeness is in the cerebellum.

The office of this organ is to lead animals and man to

FREDERICK FROEBEL.
(Founder of Kindergarten.)
PHILOPROGENITIVENESS.

PLATE XIII.

Philoprogenitiveness.   93

fully to bed, soothes its imagined distresses, she teaches it the lessons she has herself been taught, and exhorts it to obedience in the tone and manner to which she is most accustomed from her own instructor. The knowledge we communicate we fix more deeply in our own minds, and so strongly is the desire of having something to teach and something to take charge of implanted within us, that we have known a little girl who had no companions, repeat her lessons and the instructions given to herself, to a favorite rose-bush.

---

select one sexual mate, and to live faithfully with that mate for life. Some animals choose a mate for life, others select every year, but the love, and its exercise, is individual and exclusive.

Man embodies in himself all the faculties found in the lower animals, among which is the instinct for selecting and loving one beloved object. This exists in different persons in different degrees of strength; and when we find persons to whom the obligation of marriage is imprisonment, and onerous, it will be found that their selection was, in the first place, an improper one, or the person is deficient in the faculty of Conjugality.

Bigamy and polygamy are as unnatural as gluttony, theft, cowardice, instability, or the lack of any of the intellectual faculties. Men may be idiots, or very weak, in music, mechanism, finance, dignity, courage, and why not in the conjugal instinct? There are more people who can not distinguish tunes, than there are persons who do not desire to select and faithfully live with one conjugal mate. Some can not sing, cipher, or construct; some can not remember forms or faces, history, words, or colors. Why should not some lack conjugal love? For a full exposition of this interesting subject see "Thoughts on Domestic Life," by Nelson Sizer. S. R. Wells & Co., Publishers. Price, 25 cents.

It is not often considered that Philoprogenitiveness is a mere extension of the directly selfish feeling; that the overweening fondness of parents for their own children, as their *own*, is a branch of selfishness, and a powerful check upon the benevolent feelings. A most ridiculous manifestation of this feeling is the attempt at its transference to friends and visitors, and the showing-off of children before them. Aided by its strong light, a mother sees a thousand endearing characteristics in her offspring; but such attributes are exactly those which can not or ought not to be displayed. If it is a little red baby or a very young child that is expected to be admired, then the visitor is the victim; if an older child is expected to show off its pretty ways, its unconscious prettiness or virtue is transformed into a conscious one, and the child is then no longer pretty or virtuous. It is singular that all parents can see this mistake in others and yet so many practice it themselves, forgetting that Philoprogenitiveness, which is the love of our own children, does not necessarily extend in a like degree to other people's. A more serious abuse of the faculty is where the father of a family toils to provide for his children, urges forward their interest in every possible way, spends his health, his life, in securing for them a favorable station in the world, and so thinks all his duties to society fulfilled; when the mother satisfies her conscience in withdrawing from benevolent exertions, in relinquishing her place in the affections of her friends, because—" she has her family to attend to "—neither of them considering that the most valuable part of their children's education should be the witnessing of their efforts for the good of others, for the improvement of society, and promotion of general happiness. We frequently hear of a person who has thus cut herself off from all her duties to society to attend to her children, that she is a good *mother;* why so is a tigress, in precisely the same sense.

The children follow in the same course as the parents, and so the world makes little progress; nor can it be expected to make any while the main object of parents in the education of their children is—not that they may be happy themselves in making others so—but, that " they may get along in the world."

Much has been said and written about spoiling and pampering children, but we are disposed to think that there is more to fear from the opposite extreme of neglect and harshness. The great object in the management of children is to make them happy, to keep them constantly cheerful; to allow no angry passion, no depressing feeling, no fears to take possession of the mind, but to keep the perpetual sunshine of hope and love always bright and clear. This can be done only by constant occupation, not in eating or mere amusement, but in well-selected bodily and mental pursuits. Kindness and gentleness shown toward children, awaken the like in them. If anger be shown toward or before children, it arouses the same feeling in them. Firmness, not anger, is required in controlling them.

Dr. Combe, in his work on the " Management of Infancy," says: " Let us, then, not deceive ourselves, but ever bear in mind, that, what we desire our children to become, we must endeavor to be before them. If we wish them to grow up kind, gentle, affectionate, upright, and true, we must habitually exhibit the same qualities as regulating principles in our conduct, because these qualities act as so many stimuli to the respective faculties in the child. If we can not restrain our passions, but at one time overwhelm the young with kindness, and at another surprise and confound them by our caprice or deceit, we may, with as much reason, expect to 'gather grapes from thorns or figs from thistles,' as to develop moral purity and simplicity of character in them. It is vain to argue that, because the infant intellect is feeble, it can not detect the inconsistency which we practice. The feelings and reasoning faculties being perfectly distinct from each other, may, and sometimes do, act independently, and the feelings at once condemn, although the judgment may be unable to assign a reason for doing so. Here is another of the many admirable proofs which we meet with in the animal economy of the harmony and beauty which pervade all the works of God, and which render it impossible to pursue a right course without also doing a collateral good, or to pursue a wrong course without producing collateral evil. If the mother, for example, controls her own temper for the sake of her child, and endeavors systematically to seek the guidance of her higher and purer feelings in her general conduct, the good which results is not limited to the consequent improvement of the child. She herself becomes healthier and happier, and every day adds to the pleasure of success. If the mother, on the other hand, gives way to fits of passion, selfishness, caprice, and injustice, the evil is by no means limited to the suffering which she brings upon herself. Her child also suffers both in disposition and happiness; and while the mother receives, in the one case, the love and regard of all who come into communication with her, she rouses, in the other, only their fear or dislike. The remarkable influence of the mother, in modifying the disposition and forming the character of the child, has long been observed; but it has attracted attention chiefly in the instances of intellectual superiority. We have already seen that men of genius are generally descended from, and brought up by, mothers distinguished for high mental endowments. In these cases, the original organization and mental constitution inherited from the parent are no doubt chiefly influential in the production of the genius. But many facts concur to show that the fostering care of the mother in promoting the development of the understanding, also contributes powerfully to the future excellence of the child; and there is reason to believe that the predominance of the mother's influence upon the constitution of the offspring, in such cases, is partly to be ascribed to the care of the child devolving much more exclusively upon her than upon the father, during this the earliest and most impressionable period of its existence."

Again, the Rev. C. Anderson, to the same effect, says: "In their laudable anxiety, two parents, with a family of infants playing around their feet, are heard to say, 'Oh! what will, what can best educate these dear children?' I reply, Look to yourselves and your circumstances. Your example will educate them; your conversation with your friends; the business they see you transact; the likings and dislikings you express; *these* will educate them; your domestics will educate them; the society you live in will educate them; and whatever be your rank or situation in life, your home, your table, and your behavior there—*these* will educate them. To withdraw them from the unceasing and potent influence of these things is impossible, except you were to withdraw yourself from them also. Some persons talk of *beginning* the education of their children the moment they are capable of forming an idea. Their education is already begun; the education of circumstances—insensible education, which, like insensible perspiration, is of more constant and powerful effect, and of far more consequence to the habit than that which is direct and apparent. Its education goes on at every instant of time—you can neither stop it nor turn its course. Whatever these, then, have a tendency to make your children, these, in a great degree, *you*, at least, should be persuaded they will be."*

---

* This propensity is one of the most interesting subjects of study in the whole mental economy. And this interest is enhanced because of its tender, self-sacrificing nature, and because, also, it is possessed in many of the lower animals in as great a degree, and as perfect in manifestation, as it is in the best specimens of the human race.

In all sentient life, wherever the young require parental care, the parents are endowed with the faculty to just such extent and degree as the needs of the young require. Some animals and insects have enough of this endowment to lay eggs in water, sand, or elsewhere, leaving them for time and sunshine to hatch them. This being all that their young require, the parental instinct stops there. Others lay eggs and sit upon them for several weary weeks to hatch them, and then feed and brood and protect the chicks until grown. This beautiful trait of character, parental love, is not manifested in proportion to the intelligence or gentle-

ADHESIVENESS.
(FRIENDSHIP).

This is the gregarious instinct, and the tendency to attachment which is expressed by the term; it aids in the formation of society, and is the source from whence arises the particular friendships found there. When well developed, it constitutes what is called "an affectionate disposition," and causes children to nestle in their mother's lap, or sit down and lay their little heads together.

It is a mental attraction of cohesion which causes human beings to cling together and form themselves into compact bodies, acting only upon such individuals as are brought into sufficiently close contact by similarity of constitution and circumstances as to fall within its sphere. Its first and closest bond is family union, the love of brothers and sisters, and all who are in

---

ness of disposition in the animal. The tiger, the hyena, the wildcat, the wolf, the venomous serpent, with all their fierceness and cruelty, are quite as assiduous in their loving, parental tenderness, as are the rabbit, deer, or dove, which are mainly devoid of courage and cruelty.

The love of young bears no proportion to the development of the moral and intellectual powers in the human race. The "Cotter" as his children gather in of a "Saturday night," has as deep a fondness for them as it is possible for a prince to exhibit. Indeed the Carib flat-head, Indian cannibals, belonging to the lowest type of human beings so far as moral and mental power is concerned, and cruel and fierce in the last degree, are models of parental love. They defend their children with their life, and mourn immoderately if they die.

close household companionship, gradually extending to school-fellows, neighbors, and more distant acquaintances. It is a disposition always seeking to be near its object, mentally as well as corporeally; making the infant restless when removed from its nurse, and the school-girl hurt if her daily correspondent does not tell her every thought and purpose. The habits of the mind are as infectious as those of the body, and the choice of our associates becomes highly influential upon our own disposition. "Tell me a man's companions, and I will tell you what he is."

Children necessarily attach themselves strongly at first to those who minister most to their comfort and gratification (pity that parents should so often resign this advantage into other and ill-qualified hands!); but, as they become older, and better able to look beyond self, they may be led to value most as friends those who are most deserving of esteem; and even in young children it is delightful sometimes to witness the generous pride that is taken in the good qualities and dispositions of their little companions. Unless the young be led thus to discriminate, they will naturally, under the guidance of this propensity, make choice of such persons for friends who have greater number of feelings in common with themselves, or who most gratify their own feelings. Thus they may attach themselves to those who gratify their pride, or vanity, or appetite; their prodigality or senseless prejudices. When this bond of union is dissolved, and these feelings are no longer indulged, the attachment is alienated—for it is on the basis of the moral sentiments only that friendship can be permanent—but the ill effects remain.

ANNA C. M. RITCHIE.
ADHESIVENESS.
PLATE XIV.

And yet the feeling may, by judicious management, be so directed and regulated in the young as to render it impossible that they should, at any period of life, exercise it upon an unworthy object.

Under such regulation nothing can be more amiable than the manifestation of a warm, affectionate disposition, although the want of it in early childhood need not, perhaps, be the source of much anxiety. A great difference is observable in children as to the proportion of this feeling in their constitutions. One child seems as if he could not be happy for a moment without his accustomed companions; if he goes to play, they must go too; if he learns, he will do it best when they learn with him. I have known one twin brother commit the same trivial fault for which the other was suffering punishment, that he might share the penalty with him. Another child will pursue his studies and his sports alone, seemingly quite contented and happy without the sympathy of others. Some children, especially boys, will always repel caresses, and for many years wound the heart of mother and friends by an utter indifference to their affection. And yet, if the mind be well constituted in other respects, and the child happily circumstanced, better-founded affection will spring up and supply the vacuum felt in childhood. A son's love for his mother often grows out of the respect which an insight into her mind and appreciation of her character produce: consequently it is a love deeper in its nature and more capable of growth than the innate, half-animal affection which Adhesiveness generates. Hence this love is often far stronger in the man than in the boy.

The expression of a child's affection should be met by an affectionate manner in return, but merit should never be attached to its display. When the feeling seems less strong than it ought to be, it should be strengthened and cultivated by the only efficacious mode—kindness. Its outward expression even should be encouraged, as having a tendency to exercise the feeling. This outward expression, however, should never be commanded, neither should it be stimulated, as we have said, by praise, as these modes of exciting its manifestation would be liable to lead to insincerity, and render love itself false.

In the present state of society this selfish feeling too frequently takes the place and credit of benevolence. A man who, following the dictates of this propensity, is kind to and serves his immediate friends and connections, conceives that he is acting under the influence of the higher moral sentiment, and the world countenances him generally in the idea; but a much higher benevolence than this is necessary to the happiness of mankind, or even to distinguish man from the brutes; to whom also this feeling of particular attachment belongs.*

---

* To show that disinterested Benevolence is a higher trait than Adhesiveness, we only need to remember that the latter has to do with special friends and associates, and in its widest degree, the circle of our acquaintances; while the former not only embraces friends and intensifies our regard for them, but takes in, not only the whole human race, but all sentient beings.

We once examined a man in whom Adhesiveness was predominant. He was very religious, yet when his love of friends was pointed out and described, he said with tearful earnestness, "I sometimes think I would not care to go to

THE MORAL FEELINGS.

All the faculties we have described have for their object the preservation of the individual. They are instinctive impulses aiding the intellect to do that which is necessary to our existence and preservation. We possess them in common with the brute creation; although they are the substratum upon which every higher order of faculty, everything that peculiarly distinguishes man as man, is built; and it is evident that we must first take care of ourselves before we can take care of other people. No other person really could take care of us, if the instinctive promptings of these faculties did not induce us to do what was necessary for our own well-being. If, as Jeremy Bentham observes, Adam had cared more for Eve than he did for himself, and Eve more for Adam than for herself, the devil might have saved himself the trouble of the temptation, for the race would soon have come to an end. The social affections have still self for their center, the warmth and glow they excite being exclusively for *our own* family, *our own* friends. We are members, however, of a larger family; we belong to mankind—to society; and the purpose of the moral feelings is to enlarge our sphere of affection, to widen our embrace, and lead us to do that which is right and kind to all.

CONSCIENTIOUSNESS.

It is the office of this feeling to permit and sanction the action of each of the faculties so far as is consistent

---

heaven if I could not see and recognize my friends there, because without them it would not be heaven to me."

with justice, and with the rights of others. It is the source of the moral sense, or the sense of duty; its workings are conspicuous in straightforward uprightness of conduct, the nice sense of justice, the love of truth, delicacy of manners and sentiments, and that general sincerity and openness of character, which produce at once the conviction that its possessor is an honest man.

It manifests itself very early in some children, and often very powerfully. The deep blush, the look of anguish and apprehension which frequently accompany even the slightest dereliction from duty on the part of a child, testify that the moral principle within has already begun its work of checking every tendency to vice. It has been observed that "no fault is trifling in a child." We may all know by experience that no fault is trifling *to* a child. The first little sins which children commit appear to them as great in magnitude as the most outrageous crimes that disturb society; and their feeling of anguish in consequence of them is often far more intense than that experienced by the most notorious criminals. If, then, these little sins are treated with indifference, and regarded according to the mischief done by them, and not according to the relation which they bear to the character, a blow is given to the conscience which may blunt and deaden it irreparably. Great crimes are execrated and punished, although merely resulting from the same principle, acting in the same manner, which was unnoticed in childhood, because then minute in its consequences. A child's conscience tells him that he is much more guilty when he steals a gooseberry out of the garden against positive

Hon. SOLOMON FOOTE.

CONSCIENTIOUSNESS.

PLATE XV.

orders, and eats it hastily for fear of being seen, than when, in the glee of his enthusiasm, he tries his new carpenter's tools upon the mahogany table in the drawing-room. We honor the mother who feels truly most concern for the first offense. The rebuke, appealing to the reason only for the damage to the table, should be very different to the sorrowing remonstrance, and perhaps punishment, for the theft. The tone of correction should always chime in with the voice of conscience.

The moral sense is not active so early in some children as in others, and we must especially guard against making matters of conscience of very trifling things. With some parents so many things are wrong, according to the temper they are themselves in, or according to the caprice of the moment, and "naughty" is a word so often repeated, that a child's conscience is without a guide, and becomes completely bewildered. We must be careful not to call a thing wrong at one time and not at another; a child will soon detect our inconsistency. Unless we ourselves have a clear conscience— that is, clear and definite ideas of right and wrong— and unless our principles are consistent, certain, unwavering and undeviating, it is impossible that we can properly guide the conscience of a child. That of which we ourselves have any doubt, let us never make a question of conscience with a child. Let us avoid making too many direct appeals to the conscience, for that which a child does that is wrong is not often of much consequence; but when he does wrong knowing it to be so, that is of consequence.

In such a case the sense of guilt should never be suffered to wear away by time in a child's mind, no acknowledgment of it nor reparation having been made. Fénélon says: "Never tell a child of a fault without at the same time suggesting some mode of redressing it, which will induce him to put it into practice; for nothing is more to be avoided than that chagrin and discouragement which are the consequence of mere formal correction." Above all, a child should never be suffered to go to sleep upon an evil conscience. All offenses must be repaired and forgiven, and the soul at peace with itself before the eyelids close for the night. The regular habit of effacing from the mind every stain that may be incurred, by genuine penitence and heartfelt intention of amendment, has an influence which can scarcely be attained by any other means. If the conscience of the child be in itself susceptible, the confession will be voluntary; it will be felt a relief from the anguish of self-reproach, and then the happy task of the mother will be to soothe and encourage— not, be it observed, to flatter by praise of the virtuous feeling of sorrow, and thus obstruct the healthy effect by turning back its current upon itself, but by showing how the salutary pain may lead to blessed results hereafter. If, on the contrary, the sentiment of duty in a child be weak or deficient, it will be the mother's part to lead it on by gentle questioning till the fault committed is brought again clearly before the mind, and being shown in its true colors now that the excitement of passion is passed, it will awaken the consciousness of wrong that was before unfelt.

The least conscious fault should be acknowledged, and a painful impression should ever be associated with it. But here we must observe that nothing tends so completely, utterly, to destroy the moral sense as undue severity; let the pain of having done wrong be felt as sufficient punishment, if no other were to follow. For children of a more advanced age all outward punishment may be positively injurious. When the power of conscience is strong, the feelings deep, and the disposition retiring, often the less notice that is taken of a fault the better. In such a child the sense of demerit will be far stronger and the repentance more sincere, if he is treated with the same kindness and confidence as before, than if the fault be dragged into public view and he himself is treated as a criminal; for in that case the wound given to the feelings may be too deep, and good resolves may be turned in a contrary direction.

Conscientiousness is a main element of gratitude, so far as the sentiment consists in the desire to return an equivalent for the benefit received. It may be very early cultivated in the nursery by requiring from children an uniform courteous acknowledgment of the services of servants, and a return of kindness by every means in their power.

If an individual possess much Conscientiousness and Cautiousness and little Firmness in his character, he will be painfully susceptible as to the consequences of his actions, and unable to decide upon them without great hesitation and difficulty; a highly cultivated intellect can then alone prevent the conscience from becoming over-scrupulous and sickly. It is true that the world does not suffer much from over-tender consciences; but some good may be left undone through an excessive fear of doing wrong, and hence this state of mind becomes a positive evil.

But the world does suffer very much from *misdirected* consciences. The office of the feeling, as stated before, is to permit the action of each faculty only so far as is consistent with justice. Right is that which conduces to the greatest utility, and which, *all things considered*, produces most happiness; and wrong is that which produces *unnecessary* pain. But such a rule for calculating what is right, although very well for moralists to establish principles upon, and to decide between the conflicting claims of the morality of different nations and of the customs of society, is evidently beyond the reach of children; they must be taught to have faith in the dictum of their parents. This is right—that is wrong—must be sufficient for them. When an action is to be performed, it will never do to calculate consequences; then all consequences to ourselves and others must be left out of consideration in obedience to calculations previously dispassionately made, and to what we have otherwise been taught to believe is right. The first and the last question must always be, What is right? and it is the principal object of a good education to enable us at once to answer the question; for to doubt, when the feelings are engaged, is too frequently to be lost. Virtue, before it can be depended upon, must become a *habit of doing what is right*, instinctively, automatically, at once, and without calculation. Not to tell anything but the truth is always right; and in this instance, as in thousands of others equally clear, children should never be allowed to hesitate for a moment, or to think about saving themselves, or saving others, by telling what is false.

The principle of truth is more valuable than the good of any individual.

If the natural development of the moral sense be deficient, besides employing every means to strengthen it directly, we must endeavor to aid and support it by a strenuous cultivation of the religious principle. We must always bear in mind, however, in our educational treatment, that each faculty, or rather class of faculties, must be appealed to separately. It is a common error to suppose that in exercising the religious feelings, we necessarily cultivate the moral sense, for it is quite certain that the former may exist in considerable proportion in a character with a very imperfect development of the latter. Hence we sometimes find piety and zeal in the exercises of religion, accompanied by indifference as to the discharge of other and important moral duties.

While health and peace of mind reward obedience to the dictates of this faculty, the sense of guilt, repentance, and remorse, are the pains which punish opposition to them. It is needless, surely, to say that these latter feelings are not virtuous in themselves, and that they are good only in so far as they lead to amendment. The mind should never be permitted to dwell in a sense of demerit, but the feeling of having done wrong should be invariably associated with the endeavor to repair it, and the determination to amend the faulty disposition which induced it. The pains of wounded conscience, the severest man can know, are only attached to evil for the purpose of its cure.

The feeling which we are considering is the most important of all, because it regulates the proper action of all the others, by confining them within the bounds of what is right. It makes us desire "to do to others as we would they should do to us," and to love truth and sincerity above all things. It is painfully evident to all who think upon the subject, how much the world needs the proper cultivation, exercise, and direction of this faculty. It is disheartening to contemplate the vast area which " Vanity Fair " occupies, in which each acts a part, each wears a mask, each endeavors to deceive his neighbor by passing for something more or less than he is, and each is satisfied with mere seeming, without being or doing. Love of approbation is the prime mover; the craving for *distinction*, not *excellence*—to *appear*, not *to be*. Praise is the grand desideratum, and as *to be* virtuous is often too difficult or too troublesome, the semblance is assumed of whatever will best secure the approbation of society. The large development of Conscientiousness can alone counteract this wide-spreading and infectious tendency. We must strengthen the love of truth, of sincerity, of candor, in our children, and begin early to make them feel heartily ashamed of taking credit which is not strictly their due. Never neglect an opportunity of showing how mean, how dishonest it is. But how can the love of truth be best implanted, and the dishonesty of society counteracted? First, with reference to speaking the truth. The truth is not merely a literal representation, it is that which does not deceive. In early childhood it is much more easy to teach a child not to deceive than to tell the truth. A child in trying its new and first acquisition, its faculty of speech, says so much with no other purpose than the pleasure of talking;

mixes so much nonsense and pure imagination with the truth that it is vain to attempt to discriminate between fiction and falsehood, and as useless as vain. We must be very careful, therefore, how we accuse children of falsehood; we must be content to wait till they can themselves discriminate between one and the other, and, in the meantime, when their statements are very wide of facts, let us merely say, " Oh, that is nonsense, that is only fun." But as soon as we can, as soon as the proper age will permit, let us train a child on all occasions scrupulously to tell the literal truth, and teach him how to do it. This species of teaching is one of the best exercises the mind can possibly have. Language, although it is too frequently the medium of concealing our thoughts, was not, it may be presumed, given for that purpose—on the contrary, we should always endeavor that our speech should, as near as we can make it, correspond exactly to our thoughts and feelings. How little is this practiced; one-half of what almost every one says is false: that is, it does not correspond to the real state of thought and feeling, but it is said rather in obedience to the dictates of kindness or politeness, or the desire to please, to show off, and to appear clever. How often is the language of grief upon the tongue with joy sparkling in the eye, and how easy does it seem to compose almost perfect sentences expressive of condolence, of joy, or sorrow, without any real feeling whatever. We must learn to value *truth* above all things, and to do without this inconvertible currency of mere words.

Let us carefully discard the double comparatives and superlatives that now so much disfigure the language of society, and tolerate no exaggeration whatever. How much of that which is false arises from the want of not knowing really how to tell the truth, and how much from the dishonest wish to make important what we have to tell. Accustom children, therefore, to the strictest accuracy as to when, where, how, and wherefore, and teach them that it is best and most becoming to hold their tongues when an event is not of sufficient importance in itself to be mentioned, and that when it is, the object to be arrived at is not a brilliant relation, but a faithful, clear, and intelligible one. To give a leaning in our speech to the side we prefer is almost as bad as direct falsehood, and we should certainly discourage special pleading, and, as far as possible, teach children to state fairly both sides of the question. Be especially careful that servants do not teach children deceit by inducing them to keep secret what they see and hear in the nursery. Always help a child to tell the truth; for a willful lie, when detected, must be treated as the most heinous of offenses—as the meanest, the vilest, the greatest, the one never to be overlooked or disposed of without punishment.

But we must be as careful not to act a lie, as not to tell one. It will be impossible to teach truth and candor to children unless we are truthful and candid ourselves. We must avoid all kinds of double-dealings, double-meanings, reservation; we must never express pleasure at seeing a person, and the reverse behind his back. We must never join in uncharitable opinions of our neighbors. If we are accused we must meet the spirit of the accusation, and not hide behind some little flaw in the indictment; we must not show some little immaterial circumstance to be untrue, and on that account retort upon our accuser, as if the whole charge were false. If we argue, we must not, as is too frequently the case, set up some scarecrow, some dummy of our own, and having shown its unreality, triumph in consequence over our adversary. Above all, we must not *deceive* by telling the truth; this is the worst lie of all—it is betraying with a kiss. We must never promise what we can not or do not intend to perform. We must always keep our promise, whether for reward or punishment. We know how difficult it is on all occasions to decide upon the claims of truth, and to judge in what way and how far such claims can be best supported. It is true that much discretion must be used in supporting what we believe to be the truth, and as so much of error mixes with all subjects, allowance must be made for this, and due modesty used in expression; even if we know what is the truth, it is still not to be spoken at all times, but yet on no occasion must we say what is not true or countenance any kind of deception. But Conscientiousness requires honesty as well as truth; dishonesty may be said to be an acted lie. We have got so far in a moral code as an acknowledgment from the world that "honesty is the best policy;" but the world is slow to act even upon this tardy admission, and it generally gives to its honesty a most limited interpretation. Honesty is not merely the negative of robbing and stealing, but the giving to every man strictly his due. We must not rob others of their time, by want of punctuality in keeping our appointments, or by suffering them to call again and again at our door, when we might have attended to them at once. We must admit every claim that we know to be just, whether in relation to property, character, or intelligence. We must not detract from another's merit, and steal, or even withhold, his praise. We must give a candid and fair examination to views opposite to our own, before we allow ourselves to speak decidedly upon them. And above all, in measuring out what is due to others, we must never be influenced by what others may do to us, by their opinion of us or their conduct toward us. We are to do as we would be done by, not as we are done by; and if others do wrong, it is an additional reason why we should more carefully endeavor to do what is right. In thus regulating our own conduct, we are using the most direct means of cultivating the principle of right in our children. All rules and methods are at best but small adjuncts to the teachings by example, and without that example worse than vain.

It is impossible to say too much against the universal spirit of detraction, which so extensively prevails at present, that it may be said almost to be the spirit of the age. Rumor is never to be trusted—common rumor is a common liar. No statements, however gross, monstrous, false, and improbable, can be invented against an individual, that are not instantly caught up, circulated, and by the great majority believed without investigation or evidence. That such things should be stated is, ordinarily, enough to insure almost universal credit; even the judicious and charitable few, often presuming, without further evidence than "hearsay," that there must be something in such accusations; they can not be altogether invented; there is never smoke but there is fire, etc. Even those who have been the victims of this lying tendency are as ready and even more ready to fall in with it. It is gratifying to bad people to think that others are as bad as themselves; and in society generally people feel that the easiest way to raise themselves is to pull others down.

There is another untruthful tendency against which we are called upon to be on our guard, equally general, although not equally mean and low in its origin, and which is as prevalent now as it was two thousand or three thousand years ago. Mr. Grote, in his History of Greece, says: "Where there is any general body of sentiments pervading men living in society, whether it be religious or political—love, admiration, or antipathy—all incidents tending to illustrate that sentiment are eagerly believed, rapidly circulated, and (as a general rule) easily accredited. If real incidents are not at hand, impressive fiction will be provided to satisfy the demand: the perfect harmony of such fictions with the prevalent feeling stands in the place of certifying testimony, and causes men to hear them, not merely with credence, but even with delight; to call them in question and require proof, is a task which can not be undertaken without incurring obloquy." Every conscientious person, however, must be thoroughly prepared to meet such obloquy, and he can not be too skeptical with respect to views and statements thus smoothly and rapidly carried along on the broad current of public opinion. It is astonishing when once a statement is put forth as a fact which is in accordance with public sentiment, how a thousand apparently confirmatory facts spring up at once, not one of which has the least foundation in truth. The unscrupulousness of the uneducated classes, generally speaking, is almost beyond belief, and is only equaled by their credulity; and both are in proportion to their ignorance. In fact, such is the lying spirit abroad, such the tendency to detract, to exaggerate, and to embellish, that we are not justified in believing anything to another's prejudice upon mere "hearsay," and one thing is most certain, that whether we believe such rumors or not (and sometimes it is out of our power to disbelieve), we never ought to allow this belief to prejudice the accused as regards our actions, without first hearing his side of the question. We shall too often find that the accusation has no foundation whatever; and if it is true, there are frequently extenuating circumstances which will always be taken into account by every just person, who tries to believe the best he possibly can of his neighbors and wishes to do only as he would be done by.*

---

* On no faculty of the mental constitution has there been more contrariety of opinion than on that of conscience. Several writers on ethics deny the existence of a moral faculty. One explains conscience on the basis of "fear;" another on the "love of praise;" another on "sympathy;" another on "the fitness of things;" another on "imitation." Others recognize it as a special faculty of the human soul. Phrenology settles this question by the study of the brain development; and undertakes, even in a dark room, to point out the man to whom right motives and the desire for the right for its own sake, is superior to every other consideration. We once found a man of culture and talent in whom the organ of Conscientiousness showed a marked deficiency. We advised him to cultivate it, and be careful to think of the question of right or wrong in all

BENEVOLENCE.

The object or final cause of Creation seems to be the happiness of created intelligences. The wisdom of the Creator is evidenced in the design displayed in the universe. Design means the adaptation of means to a particular purpose or end, and we must know what that purpose is before we can say that the means used to carry it out are adapted to the purpose, that is, before we can say that there is wisdom displayed in the arrangement. We must make up our minds, therefore, upon the objects of creation before we can say that wisdom is displayed in them. If it be denied that the final cause of creation is happiness, we ask what other object can there be? It is said, "the glory of God;" but a world without consciousness, or with a miserable consciousness, would be no glory to God. It is also said the object of creation is "action," and the "development of mind;" but mere action could as well exist in a world devoid of all spirit or consciousness, and we can not conceive of any use in increased development of mind, unless it led to increased happiness. If it led to misery, such increased development of mind would be worse than useless; if to indifference, it would be the same as a mere increased development of matter.

Thought is said to be "higher far than happiness," but thought that does not lead to the increase of hap-

---

his conduct. He replied, "I never did wrong in my life." We replied that if he had Conscientiousness large he would never utter such a remark, although in such a case his general conduct would be much more likely to be correct than at present with the deficiency of conscience.

piness is worse than uselessly employed. The object
of thought is to direct and guide all our faculties toward their legitimate gratification, and that legitimate
gratification it is that constitutes happiness. It is believed that happiness is allied to pleasure, and that
pleasure is only derived from the exercise of the lower
or animal propensities, but the shortest and most correct definition of happiness is, that it consists of the
sum or aggregate of pleasurable sensation from *whatever* source derived. The happiness derived from the
lower feelings is perhaps more intense than that derived
from the higher, but it is more fleeting, and more mixed
with pains. Every joy has its shadow, intense in proportion to its solidity, and such appears to be the
necessary law of human nature, that whatever increases
our capacity for joy, increases also our capacity for sorrow. There are those who deny that there is any happiness here, and that it is only in the higher pursuits of
another world that we can look for it; but in the pursuit of truth, love, and beauty, is there no happiness
here? and can any one say what is higher? Yes, to
erring creatures, the path of duty is higher. But is
not the path of duty the path of the highest happiness?
To a highly organized human being there is no happiness out of it, only deep sorrow and remorse; and the
very pains of the path of duty are joys, so much does
the higher nature transcend the lower. A Regulus had
infinitely more joy than Nero, although his higher attributes ultimately led to his confinement in the barrel
pierced with spikes. Sorrow and sadness are often only
the shortest road to the greatest gladness, and in the
regions of faith and hope, through which that path leads,

C. C. TRACY.

BENEVOLENCE.

PLATE XVI.

will be found "the peace of God which passeth all understanding," which is the highest and most enduring happiness of all. Religion is not unsatisfied yearning and aspiration, but action in the path of that duty for which we were created, and trust in God for the final accomplishment of all which our highest yearning and aspiration can not reach.

It appears to us, then, that the existence of God is proved by the evidence of design—that is, that Nature, in carrying out her endless purposes, is working toward a particular object, and that that object is happiness. "That God willed the happiness of His creatures, is indisputable; and He has made it impossible that they should not endeavor to obtain it. To this end He has given them every faculty they possess.* Here is evidence of the benevolent intentions of our Creator, and the means He adopts to carry out His intention indicate a power and wisdom far surpassing our comprehension. What more is requisite for a rational faith? God wills the happiness of His creatures, and He has power and wisdom to accomplish His wishes. May we not, therefore, safely trust in Him; may we not safely leave our fate, where, beyond our own control, whether it relates to coming into this world or going into another, in His hands? Happiness we believe to be "our being's end and aim," and it is the faculty of Benevolence which places us in harmony with this principal object in creation, and which makes us desire the happiness of others, and gives us a lively sympathy with the enjoyment of all created beings. In this, at least, it is our privilege

---

* Bentham.

to be made in the likeness of God; and as an humble instrument in aiding Him in producing happiness, and in our sympathy with it will be found our own highest enjoyment. This feeling has received various names: it is called love of mankind, goodness of heart, good nature, etc.; and joined to Conscientiousness, it constitutes that charity so beautifully described by St. Paul in the thirteenth chapter of Corinthians. As its object is to produce happiness in others, so whenever the feeling is strong in any mind, it produces happiness to its possessor, diffusing a genial warmth and sunshine through the mind, which all the frosts and clouds of life can not dispel; and as it is so powerful a diffuser of happiness, it is most important that we should attend to its early cultivation.

Each propensity, sentiment, and intellectual faculty should be put under the guidance of this desire for universal good; and let us not mistake the love which proceeds from Adhesiveness, which might more properly be called affection, for this feeling; the one relates only to individuals, the other regards the whole human race, or rather the whole sensitive creation.

Education, if rightly understood, is that mode of treatment which will teach an individual to feel, to think, and to act, so as to produce most happiness to himself and others. He must not only *know how*, but he must also be *disposed* to act. Now the disposition to act for our own good is already strong enough, as all the propensities tend to that end; but the disposition to act for the good of others depends very much upon the feeling of Benevolence.

As an instinct, it is held by some to be possessed, in

a degree, by many of the inferior animals; however this may be, its manifestations in man are often simply instinctive. It then forms the character of the good-natured man, who is impelled by it to gratify the wishes of everybody around him, if it be in his power, even at the expense of their future good. He can not say "No," and he therefore yields to the importunities of the idle and dissolute that which perhaps is due in justice to claims which are, at the moment, out of sight. He spoils his children; yielding to their entreaties, he gives what he knows to be improper for them, because, "bless their little hearts," he can not bear to hear them cry. If he threatens, he can not find strength of character to perform; if he does punish them, he tries to make amends for it, and to conciliate them by lavishing upon them extraordinary gratifications and luxuries. To diffuse immediate happiness upon those near at hand, without reference to future and more permanent good, is the short-sighted object of the uncultivated feeling of Benevolence.

When cultivated, but with a wrong direction, its operation is still of the same kind, but more mischievous as it is exerted through a wider sphere. Many of the wide-spread charities of the present day furnish examples of this. They seek to remedy a present evil, to relieve a present suffering, by means which multiply for the future these pains and sufferings many fold. A late writer on the principles of Charitable Institutions remarks, that they are more numerous, that more exertions are made for the relief of the poor now than at any former period, yet poverty and crime are on the increase. What is the reason of this? The writer alluded to goes on to prove that it is to be found in the fact, that remedies are often applied without discriminating between the different causes which produce these evils, and therefore perpetuate and increase them, or at best only palliate them. But the real cause of this want of discrimination and consequent failure is the fact that it is not real benevolence at work, but a something between the *seeming* of love of approbation and a bargain to get as cheaply as possible to heaven. People wish to stand well in the opinion of their neighbors, and they have likewise heard that "he that giveth to the poor, lendeth to the Lord," and they approve of the security and invest a small sum, but never more than they can conveniently spare; to do more would be imprudence! They do their charities, that is, give annual guineas, the press generally blowing a trumpet before them; but they neither watch the spending of the money nor care much what becomes of it—consequently, the more remote the sphere of operation—if to build a Church at Jerusalem for converted Jews, or to make Christians of Caribs—the more liberal the donation. Children should be early taught to distinguish between seeming and real benevolence—between generosity that costs nothing, that is, involves no self-sacrifice or even self-denial, and that which proceeds from love and duty. When the higher classes are really in earnest about raising the condition of the lower—when they cease to consider them as mere objects to perform their charities upon, as convenient stepping-stones to heaven, as so much raw material out of which they are to work their own salvation, as *the poor*, "whom we are always to have with us," and therefore are to be kept poor, or at least in their present position as lower orders—then there will be less difficulty in removing the artificial and ultimately the natural barriers to their success. A little well-directed effort to do good is better than a large and expensive beneficence on a wrong principle.

That which is commonly called charity, the succoring and aiding of distress, is but a limited exercise of benevolence; but that which Paul denominates charity is the true, divine Spirit of Love—" Though I should give all my goods to feed the poor, and have not charity, I am nothing,"—that charity which "loveth all things" and which strives to add to the enjoyment of every living creature within its reach.

If a child be introduced to the instances of benevolent design throughout the universe, he can not but perceive that the purpose of its Creator is the production of the largest possible sum of enjoyment, that the apparent exceptions to this must arise from our limited knowledge, and that earth, air, and sea are full of innumerable creatures all practically praising their Maker, by their sense of this enjoyment that He has given them; and a child's natural sympathy with what is good and beautiful will soon excite the desire to use his own little powers to the furtherance of the same object. The desire will grow with its indulgence, and with the development of these powers, until he will have no idea of happiness except as associated with the happiness of others. Thus, if we wish to create in our child a liberal spirit, extended sympathies, a loving disposition, "identify him," says Richter, "with the life of others, and give him a reverence for life under every form: teach him to consider all animal life as sacred. . . . .

"You may teach a higher than Ovid's Art of Love, by requesting your child to do something without commanding or rewarding performance, or punishing neglect; only depict beforehand, if it is for another, or afterward if for yourself, the pleasure which the little actor's attention to your wish affords. You excite the Benevolence of children less by pictures of people's necessities than of the joy produced by relieving them. For the little heart conceals so great a treasure of love, that he is less deficient in willingness to make sacrifices than in the certainty that they would give pleasure. Hence, when children have once begun to make presents they would never cease giving. The parents may give the reward of certain happiness by a gladly praising approval; an educational lever whose power has not been sufficiently estimated. For children accustomed only to parental bidding and forbidding, are made happy by permission to do some extra service, and by the recognition of their having done it. This affectionate acknowledgment of pleasure renders them neither vain nor empty, but full—not proud, but warm.

"It does the poor man, or dog, or whatever it may be, good, or harm! These few words, said in a proper tone of voice, are worth a whole sermon: and fie! said to a girl, will abundantly fill the place of half a volume of 'Ehrenberg's Lectures to the Female Sex.'

"Do not apprehend too great danger to the affections from children's quarrels. Their incapacity to place themselves in another's position, and their Adam-like innocence of belief that the whole world is made for them, and not they for the world; all these things combine to raise the inflated bubbles which soon break of themselves. They may speak harshly, or even fly into a passion with one another, but must not continue it! You must do many more things to be hated than to be loved by children : hated parents must themselves have hated for a long time. Advancing years rarely awaken a repressed or dormant love; the individual's own selfishness doubles that of others, and this again redoubles that; and so layer upon layer of ice is frozen. You falsify love by commanding its outward expression; kissing the hand, for instance. Such things, unlike kind actions, are not the causes, but only the effects of love. Do not in any instance require love : among grown-up persons would a declaration of affection, if commanded and prescribed by the highest authorities, be well received?

"And finally, ye parents, teach to love, and you will need no ten commandments; teach to love, and a rich winning life is opened to your child; for man (if this simile be permitted) resembles Austria, which increases its territory by marriage, but loses its acquisitions by war; teach to love, in this age, which is the winter of time, and which can more easily conquer everything than a heart by a heart; teach to love, so that when your eyes are old, and their sense almost extinguished, you may yet find around your rich couch and dying bed no greedy covetous looks, but anxious weeping eyes, which strive to warm your freezing life, and lighten the darkness of your last hour by thanks for their first. Teach to love, I repeat; that means—do you love!"* †

---

* Levana.
† Perhaps one of the best methods for the improvement

THE ÆSTHETIC FEELINGS.

By the Æsthetic is meant the sense of the beautiful and sublime, the love of art and poetry, the feeling of the spiritual element in all the various forms of art, the desire of the soul for the perfect. Ideality is the only sentiment we have placed under that head, not because it is alone essential to the formation of the æsthetic character of mind, but because it constitutes its foundation.

---

of the faculty of Benevolence, is for a person to seek out some one who is poorer than himself, and take his interests in hand with a view to their improvement. He will soon find that in doing good there is great recompense of joy. If one feels poor and discouraged, let him go through some of the streets of a great city which are the abode of the very poor, and he will soon learn to be grateful for the blessings which crown his own life, and at the same time profoundly moved to sympathy in behalf of those whose life is a grievous struggle and a burden. The rich who have opportunity to enjoy all that study, travel, art, and society can bestow, are apt to become selfish and ungrateful in the midst of plenty; they fret at the weather or anything else that may interfere with their search after pleasure. The greatest blessing some people ever receive, comes in the form of disaster to their worldly prosperity, and the humbling of the attendant pride and selfishness. It brings them to their better selves, to the exercise of their higher powers, and they might say with the psalmist, "Before I was afflicted I went astray, but now have I kept Thy word. It is good for me that I have been afflicted, that I might learn Thy statutes."

IDEALITY.

It is difficult to say what is the primitive function of this faculty; it is easier to say what are its results in combination with other faculties—that is, what it leads to. Viewed philosophically, man must not be regarded as a mere present individual, but must be looked at in his relation to the past, the present, and the future. From the past he has received the results of the experience of by-gone ages, and, in consequence, is a recipient of the benefits of an advanced civilization; in the present he is called upon to perform his little part in the chain of causation, but in doing this it behooves him not to rest satisfied with the material comforts and pleasures which past generations have prepared for him, but to do also his part toward promoting the interests of the future; he is bound to leave the generation which is to follow him benefited by his existence, as he has been benefited by the one preceding him. That he may do this, it is essential that he should not rest satisfied with the perfection that breathes around him, but that he should always aspire to something higher and better, and aim to give it being.

Ideality gives the desire to do this, and upon this feeling is based the progressive character of man's existence, and the perfectibility of his nature. Nature seems to aim here at the perfection of the race, not of individual man. So far as we regard man as the inhabitant of this earth, he is the temporary receptacle of high spiritual attributes—of mental manifestations. The individual passes away, but Youth and Beauty and Delight are immortal; as the poet says, "For them there is no death nor change." Through a series of generations mind is developed, great principles are worked out, and become more strongly marked—truth and goodness and holiness and beauty have a larger and stronger and more forcible existence, although the material organization by which this development has been effected has passed away like the leaves in autumn. Ideality, then, is the desire for, and the consequent striving after, an ideal perfection—that is, a perfection greater than we find existing; it is a dissatisfaction with the present and the actual, and the yearning after a future state in which everything will be perfect. The mode in which this feeling manifests itself, of course, depends upon the other feelings and intellectual faculties with which it is allied; as we have said before, it gives rise to the æsthetic part of our nature, to poetic feeling, and to the love of the beautiful. We have heard those in whom the feeling was strong, say that it seemed to give to everything a double existence—to that which would otherwise be mere material things with material uses, it endows with high and spiritual attributes. For instance, to a person without this feeling, the Venus de Medicis would be a mere " stone gal," as the rustic called it, while to another differently endowed, it would be the ideal or perfection of physical beauty. If we examine to ascertain in what real poetry consists, we shall find that it is the addition of this spiritual attribute of beauty and perfection to material existences. Thus poetry is principally made by adjectives, characterizing and qualifying and idealizing and beautifying the noun. For example:

FITZ-GREENE HALLECK.

IDEALITY.

PLATE XVII.

" The *breezy* call of *incense-breathing* morn,
  The swallow twittering from the *straw-built* shed,
The cock's *shrill clarion*, and the *echoing* horn,
  No more shall rouse them from their *lowly* bed."

And again:

"I have bedimmed
The *noontide* sun, called forth the *mutinous* winds,
And 'twixt the *green* sea and the *azure* vault
Set *roaring* war."

We know every one has his definition of poetry, and every one his own idea of what is poetry. It is said to be the language of all the feelings when highly excited, that is, when they approach to passion; but it may be said rather to be the language of every feeling when under the influence of ideality, its mode of expression depending entirely upon the various combinations of the intellectual faculties. Ideality is not the same as imagination or fancy, imagination being merely a mode of action—a degree of activity of the other faculties; Ideality may excite imagination and fancy, but of itself it is a feeling, sentiment, or wish; a love of perfection for its own sake, in the same way as there is also a love of knowledge for its own sake. It has always a refining tendency, and gives an innate shrinking from all that is low and vulgar and coarse. The beautiful everywhere is its food, is that which calls it into activity, and constitutes its enjoyment. God has made everything so beautiful here that one abuse of it consists in looking to another world only for its gratification.

Ideality gives not only soul to poetry and romance, but to the prosaic concerns of every-day life. It may

6*

be called an additional sense, and no station in life necessarily debars us from its pleasures, which, like those of the other senses, ought to be common to all, and be cultivated and improved by all. Wherever there is Nature, there is beauty—wherever there is man, there should be the faculty to admire; the "privileged classes" have secured to themselves many of the means of its gratification, but they can not monopolize "the glory in the grass, the sunshine on the flower."

In order to cultivate the faculty, it is not necessary to fill the mind with the false associations and coloring of romance, or to study the models of classical antiquity; but to "go forth into Nature's school," and there it will educate itself, amidst flowers and fields, among the hills, and by the river-side. In towns and cities the lessons of Nature are more faint and few, but even here, her sunbeams gild the tops of the spires, and sparkle on the flood which reflects, as it passes by, the crowded habitations; here, too, the taste may be more readily nurtured upon the beautiful in art and science.

"Children are often very poetical. 'Are you glad that God has made it all so beautiful?' said a child to me as I was watching the sun sinking into the waves at B. The mind of another child of between four and five years old is not less imaginative. During a walk on a fine December day, it was delightful to see how happy and observing he was, stooping to look at the mosses, and to gather specimens of the few remaining plants, and talking all the way—'Look at those rainbows on the hills!' cried he, pointing to the different shades of trees, blended in the mists. He gathered a little piece of beautiful moss, and called it his forest; and took up the idea with delight, when it was suggested, that in that forest all 'the lions and tigers and wolves should play with the lambs, and little children should lead them.'—' And the little baby-boys,' he added, ' should be nursed by elephants, and the lions should put brass upon their claws, for fear of hurting the lambs.' He was told that they could make their paws soft when they liked—so he carried his jungle full of elephants and tigers carefully home, in his little cold hand. The first-mentioned of these children, when four years old, while walking in the wood at ——, wished to gather some flowers for his mamma, who was going away. 'There is no time now,' said some one present, 'but you can send her a nosegay in a few days.' 'They will hang their heads,' said he, 'when mamma goes—they will cry—they will all wither and waste away!' One evening, while watching the sunset, he said, ' The sun sinks behind the deep hills.' When four years old he would amuse himself for hours by drawing lines, and making stories about these lines; for example, 'Here is a steamboat and here is a little boat, and it goes wave, wave, wave.' But there is no good thing on this earth which may not be perverted, by excess, into bad; his imagination often leads him into untruth. When three years old he said, so very gravely, that had you only looked at his countenance, and not heard his words, you would have felt sure he believed the truth of what he was speaking.—'Do you know, just now I saw a pig walking along the road with a bonnet on?' Every day, about this time, the habit of telling falsities of this kind grew upon him. Probably he did not wish to deceive; the images passed through his mind, and he wished to communicate them, and knew not yet how to do so but by saying, 'I saw,' 'There was,' and the like forms of expression. However, *had* he meant to cheat, it is a fearful thing to begin with a child upon the subject of untruth, and the plan we pursued from the beginning was not to take the slightest notice of these effusions. To laugh at them would have been fatal, to frown on them scarcely less so; therefore there was no other course left than to remain deaf to him. Tempted on by his imagination, he still tells stories of this kind; but surely these stories are of a very different nature from those which are uttered to screen the teller from punishment."*

If the taste be nurtured upon the beautiful objects and elevated subjects which Nature presents to it, there will be no danger of its becoming sickly and distorted, by being permitted to indulge in the delights of fiction. A pure natural taste will repel all that is incongruous, and assimilate nothing but that which is pure and simple in itself.

Ideality is a strong guardian of virtue; for they who have tasted its genuine pleasures can never rest satisfied with those of mere sense. But it is possible, however, to cultivate the taste to such a degree as to induce a fastidious refinement, when it becomes the inlet of more pain than pleasure. Nor is the worst of over-refinement the loss of selfish gratification; it is apt to interfere with benevolence, to avoid the sight of inele-

---

* Monthly Repository.

gant distress, to shrink from the contact of vulgar worth, and to lead us to despise those whose feeling of taste is less delicate and correct than our own. If the beautiful and the useful be incompatible, the beautiful must give way—as the means of the existence and comfort of the masses must be provided before the elegancies which can conduce only to the pleasure of the few. Selfishness, though refined, is still but selfishness, and refinement ought never to interfere with the means of doing good in the world as it at present exists.

It is not desirable to appeal early to this feeling, or perhaps ever directly to cultivate it. If the other faculties are well developed and properly cultivated, this will attain sufficient strength of itself. The beautiful is the clothing of the infinite, and in the contemplation of the beautiful, and the love of perfection, we seek our highest and most intimate communion with God, and draw nearer and nearer to Him.

The fine arts—painting, sculpture, music, as well as poetry—ought all to minister to Ideality. The proper use of painting, for instance, ought to be to represent everything that is beautiful in the present, and to recall all that is worthy of remembrance in the past. To give body to those spiritual pictures of ideal beauty and perfection which Ideality forms—to give a faithful representation of the great and good that have departed, and to put vividly before us those actions and scenes, those pages from universal history which have a tendency to refine, to exalt, and to enlarge the soul—this is what painting ought to aim at. To paint, however perfectly, horses being shod, deer being hunted, the agony of poor animals in traps, bread and cheese, and lobsters, and foaming ale, is but an abuse and a perversion of one of the highest gifts and attainments, which a more civilized age will repudiate. A pig-stye, however perfectly painted, still but recalls the idea of a pig-stye: and if it excites any feeling, it is one of regret that such wonderful art should be so misapplied.*

THE RELIGIOUS FEELINGS.

VENERATION.

This feeling originates the disposition to respect and revere whatever is great and good and superior to ourselves; and whatever we are brought up to consider great and good and worthy of honor. According to these imbibed notions, it may be directed to rank, titles, ancestry, wealth, particular creeds and customs, laws

---

* If one will look at any garment or structure, he will be astonished to see how much of the work bestowed upon it was inspired by the faculty of Ideality. One-half the material and at least two-thirds of the work on a lady's dress, are in response to the sense of beauty. Look at the carvings, the moldings, the fine wood and trimmings which enter into the composition of the furniture of a single well-furnished room! Observe the architectural decoration of the house inside and out, the moldings, cornices, the paneling, the mantels, the frescoes, the elegant staircases; and then the curtains, carpets and upholstery, and tell us if three-fourths of all you see would not come under the head of decoration. We feel that we can not do without something in this line, and realize that

"A thing of beauty is a joy forever."

BISHOP G. D. CUMMINS.

VENERATION.

PLATE XVIII.

and institutions: or it may be attached to those objects, persons, and institutions, most worthy from their real greatness and goodness to excite respect and reverence. Hence its right direction is highly important; for whatever may be its objects, it is very difficult in after life to break the association between them and the feeling, though reason may plainly point out the absurdity of the connection, and the small inherent claim to our respect they may possess.

The feeling is an important auxiliary in moral training. Mr. Combe says: "It is the chief ingredient in filial piety, and produces that soft and almost holy deference with which a child looks up to its parent, as the author of his days, the protector of his infancy, and the guide of his youth." It constitutes part of the charm of social intercourse, as the source of the honor we pay to age, to talent, to virtue; and it connects us by a pleasing chain with all that is or has been great and good in the moral and material world.

In education the feeling has generally been drawn upon too largely, as it has been the means of attaching undue importance to antiquity and authority, considered independently of their real claims to respect; but it must not be undervalued because it has been abused, and if it be deficient in a child, it must be cultivated by directing his attention to that which is really worthy of his reverence; at the same time showing that *we* also venerate the objects which we would have him honor; for the influence of example is particularly strong over this faculty. Nothing is more chilling to this feeling than derision and ridicule; that which a child hears laughed at by others, he can never respect, so that it is necessary most carefully to exclude all such associations with that which should be held by him in esteem and reverence.

As the love we bear to our fellow-creatures is the same sentiment which with a higher direction we entertain towards our Creator, so this feeling of veneration not only originates respect to human superiority, but is the source of the disposition to the worship and adoration which is paid to the Great First Cause. It is expressed by the sacred writers in their injunctions to "Fear God," which allude to the exercise of this sentiment of deference or veneration towards Him. Thus it constitutes a large proportion of the Religious Feelings. It is on this subject that most anxiety has been felt by parents, and on which the greatest mistakes have been committed. The idea that the religious feelings proceed from supernatural influences only, and the consequent neglect of their natural culture, have occasioned a great want of success in their development and guidance. We ask for "daily bread," but we do not expect that it will be given without the exercise of the means which God has appointed to obtain it. Why then, when we pray that His "kingdom may come," do we not study the natural means appointed no less to bring it about, but sit down contented with the idea that the "kingdom of God in the heart" is only to be established by direct supernatural influence upon it? If we examine into the nature of our constitution, we shall see that certain feelings are given to us, upon the strength of which will depend the sense of religion and the disposition to perform religious duties. The most direct means to inspire a proper sense of religion, and the means which God himself has pointed out, is the strengthening of these feelings. This is the soil from whose insufficient cultivation so much of "the seed" which is sown brings forth no fruit. It has been from the neglect of these means, of the like natural means which we take to procure our "daily bread," that the spirit of religion so little prevails—that religious teachings, in general, tend to the spread of fanaticism and mere sectarianism, or to leave the mind in indifference.

Precepts alone, as we have formerly observed, have no direct tendency to strengthen the feelings, nor are they more effectual to this end in the shape of creeds and catechisms. Previous moral training is necessary to render religious instructions availing. If the feelings to which the hopes and fears of religion are addressed, and on which the love and fear of God and the Christian virtues depend, be already cultivated, then, and only then, will its appeals be really successful. From the want of this cultivation, though the cry of religion is heard on every side, the world is still in bondage to those evils which it seems to have been the special object of Christianity to remove. The grades of society are, perhaps, even more marked; the want, wretchedness, and consequent vice of the masses as prevalent, while the direct and plain precepts of Christ are disregarded, or explained away to suit the low standard of conventional moral feeling.

It is sometimes a matter of much difficulty with thoughtful parents how to deal judiciously with the tender germs of religious perception; how to strengthen, without injuring by false and unworthy association. It is a question whether it be safe to present any definite idea of God to the infant mind—whether the name and all that tends to individualize this mightiest conception of the mature mind should not be kept back until such time as the heart and understanding demand this background and solution of the world without and the world within. That God is, is the one fixed idea which sustains our humanity—the dorsal column to which, consciously or unconsciously, are firmly knit the hopes and fears, sense of security, faith in results, which are inherent to the thinking being. *What* God is, is a question that fashions itself according to each man's mode of thought at the time being. The impressions in childhood being especially vivid, there is danger that degrading images stamped then on the mind may long hamper and infect it. A child can never rest in an abstract idea or sentiment; he immediately personifies; and in this case for any human intelligence to personify, is to falsify. As the spiritual nature advances, the existence of God is capable of becoming a reality to us through His attributes, and the idea of person is less and less necessary to our conception of His being. Is it wise, then, to suffer a child to cloud his young brain and sully his imagination with wild and puerile fancies which, in after years, will be so much dust and cobweb before his mental vision? Notice the kind of impression which the religious teaching of the nursery often makes upon a child from two to five years old. He talks and asks about God in the midst of his gambols without the slightest reverence, and with a mischievous gusto, because it makes nurse look mysterious and shocked; his prayers are a sort of game, till nurse makes them a most irksome task by requiring him to look grave and keep still while he says them. Soon this prankishness may be subdued and the child may become outwardly decorous, and parents who believe religious education to consist in saying prayers and catechisms, behaving well at church, reading the Bible and being quiet on Sundays, may feel quite satisfied. Meanwhile, if children could give correct utterance to their fancies, it would be curious to know the various pictures of God which such teaching forms in their minds. Often the notion is of a colossal human being sitting on a throne, with his eyes constantly fixed on them. In one child it was an uninviting old man, perpetually employed in making men, women, and children out of dust and throwing them down to the earth as soon as they were done. In another, it was a great eye, blue and glassy, ever pursuing her; another child used to imagine an eye looking fixedly at her through a crack in the ceiling. It is related of Dr. Doddridge that his mother taught him the Old and New Testaments from the Dutch tiles in the chimney, and accompanied her instructions with such wise and pious reflections as made a lasting impression on his mind. We fear the Dutch-tile association often outlasts the wise reflections.

Zschokke remarks, "Nothing in the Christian world has so greatly contributed to the decline of Christianity as the reigning practice of imparting the higher ideas of religion to children at an age when their memory only, and not their understanding, is capable of receiving them; and in which a solemn and touching office has been degraded to a merely social custom, mechanically partaken of from habit and decorum."

Much depends in religious teaching on the natural

constitution. In children of a loving nature and poetical temperament, the idea of the Father in Heaven may be very early introduced; but to one of a timid, cold, and literal nature, we should be very cautious in the use of any image whatever to convey a notion of the Divine Being; such a child should be led to its Creator gradually, and through the medium of the understanding; the great idea should grow with its growth. The sense of a God may exist in the mind before the idea takes name and shape, and the germ of holy affections accompany the love of nature, the love of fellow-beings, and the principle of right. In a child's introduction to the natural world everything should form a lesson tending to raise and strengthen the feeling of love to nature's God. The order, the properties, the beautiful adaptation of all things to our happiness should be explained, and in proportion as these are seen and understood, the feeling of love to the Author of all the good around him, and the source of all his own comforts and happiness, must grow in the mind of a child. The mind thus daily, hourly exercised, there can be no difficulty in making the idea of the kindest and best of Beings the most interesting and delightful a child can entertain.

The ordinary mode of introducing the idea of God differs much from this. It is forgotten that a child can not love, unless the object be of such a nature as to excite his affection, and unless his heart be open to the sentiment. "The impressions made upon the minds of children concerning the Deity are generally painful, for His power is much more dwelt upon than His goodness,

The Religious Feelings.

and they are more liable to be affected by the former than the latter."

The time, and the manner, also, in which the idea is commonly presented to the minds of children, tend greatly to increase the sensation of fear, and to exclude the feeling of love. Whenever they have done wrong, and consequently are wretched and uncomfortable, they are told that God sees them and will punish them. Here is their terror through Cautiousness excited by the ideas of His omniscience and power, but no love. Whenever religious subjects are mentioned before them, they are reminded that they must be serious, which, when required, is always irksome to children, and not laugh and play because He is such an awful Being; hence they conclude that He does not like to see them happy, and that His service is a restraint. And again, it is made an imperative duty to thank Him for the past day, and to ask His protection for the night, when they are tired and sleepy, and, perhaps, shivering with cold, and the idea of devotion is necessarily associated with irksomeness and fatigue. The abuse of an excellent custom is here alluded to, not the custom itself, which is one of the happiest that the affection of a mother could devise for the cultivation of the highest and best feelings in her child. The association of bodily comfort should be made with that exercise of the mind, which reviews the blessings of the past day toward itself and others, while it renews its aspirations after improvement. The attendance of children is sometimes required at long religious services not in any way adapted to their feelings and capacities, and therefore far more wearisome than profitable to them; and while the day chiefly devoted to to these is, or ought to be, a season of peace and refreshment to their elders, to children it is too often one of tedium and dullness. They can not long be inactive and happy, and it can not be the intention of Him who gave them their buoyant, restless energies, that they should fret against each other or become torpid, for want of proper exercise, under the idea of serving Him.

Painful sensations are much more powerful than pleasurable ones, and, therefore, if fear be excited, great care should be taken that there be sufficient love to balance it. Hence, if children be reminded of God when they are faulty and uncomfortable, much more should they be reminded of Him when they are good and happy, and, if possible, let the first impulse of devotion spring spontaneously from the gratitude of the soul. Miss Hamilton tells us that she remembers, when a very young child, thanking God fervently for the pleasure she had had in dancing at a children's ball; and a little friend of ours, on finding a cherished doll which had been searched for anxiously many hours, clasped her little hands together, and with the most grateful fervor exclaimed, "Good God, I thank thee!" No matter what the occasion of the feeling, the feeling itself in both these cases puts to shame the prayers which many children are made to repeat, parrot-like, night and morning, under the superintendence of the nursemaid, and associated with nothing but that which is chilling and disagreeable. If parents were really as anxious that their children should love God, as that they should love themselves, they would use the same means for exciting this love; they would not so much enforce it as a duty that He should be loved and thanked, as to lead the child to do so of his own accord; they would endeavor that He should be associated in their minds with every idea of cheerfulness and enjoyment, and thus lay the foundation for a pure, rational, and efficient religious principle.*

---

* Not only the *language* of the sacred Scriptures, but also that of religious teaching, and the sacred poetry and prayers, as well as the idea of God's government as set forth in theological works, appear to have largely grown out of or to have been suggested by the prevalent kingly governments among men. As the king was the highest ideal of power, and a throne the highest imaginable earthly attainment, and as kingly power in early times was very absolute, it was quite natural that God should be called a king and His government regarded as a manifestation of absolute power. In the days of the prophets kings were feared and dreaded by the people. The will and word of the king carried life or death, sometimes without justice or reason. Such, then, was the idea of human government, and it is not strange that men, so trained to fear sovereignty, should thus be led to regard God as an infinite sovereign, imbued with all the tyranny and capricious vindictiveness belonging to those high ideals of earthly power, yet enhanced to an infinite degree. This dread, sovereign power, was called God's glory. He was frequently called the God of battles, and spoken of as having fury, vengeance and hatred. They would naturally worship this almighty power, and be likely to forget His goodness. Under such ideas of God, the people would learn to fear and dread the Creator, and exercise the faculty of Veneration in a manner foreign to the real principle of God-worship. Even the psalmist, in a moment of ecstasy breaks forth, "Do not I hate them,

HOPE.

It is the privilege of the inferior animals to suffer no pain beyond that of the present moment, to anticipate no evil; it is the higher privilege of man to look forward in present ill to future good, to feel during the fury of the storm the influence of the coming sunshine. Religion, philosophy, poetry, have united to class Hope among the higher principles of our nature, as the support to piety, the element of cheerfulness, the balm of human woes; but we must not confound that exercise of the feeling which is purely instinctive and directed toward a determinate object, distinct and bright, though distant, with that arising from its cultivation as a moral feeling. The former will create a sanguine and cheerful temper, prone to rise when the immediate pressure

---

O Lord, that hate thee? I hate them with a perfect hatred."

Do we ever think that the same idea of God pervades sacred poetry of a later date? Take the popular and familiar stanza,

"Before Jehovah's *awful* throne,
Ye nations *bow* with sacred joy;
Know that the Lord is God alone,
He can create and He *destroy!*"

The prevalent idea of God seems to be Sovereignty, power! But other sentiments here and there find expression, which are more in harmony with true veneration and the spirit of the other moral and religious faculties. For instance, "As a father pitieth his children, so the Lord pitieth them that fear him."

In a semi-barbarous people, to whom war and conquest were the high ideal of government and nationality, the

THOMAS RIVERS.

HOPE.

PLATE XIX.

of suffering is taken off—and this is in a measure valuable; but the latter alone will enable the mind to seek for objects of consolation in the midst of pain and distress, to turn the attention from what has been taken away to what is left, and to remember that "though sorrow may endure for a night, joy cometh in the morning." It is only when cultivated that the natural feeling of hope, which gives vigor and animation to the season of childhood and youth, can become a permanent and elevating principle of mind.

The first practical lesson which a mother can give to her child on this subject is her own habitual cheerfulness; long before it can be understood in words it can be felt by sympathy; her cheerful tone and manner will often dispel the infant's rising tear and convert it

---

sovereignty and power of kings would color their religious as well as social and governmental ideas.

So long as the young are taught first and chiefly of the power, majesty and vengeance of the Almighty, and little or nothing of His fatherhood, it is not strange that all their ideas of worship are born of fear rather than of filial love. Hence it is, that nine-tenths of the religious conversation and prayers of Christian people, are addressed to Jesus the loving Saviour and "Prince of peace," and but for whose constant pleadings and intercessions, they seem to think, an angry God would instantly smite and destroy mankind. The truth is, we are taught to *love* Christ and to *fear* God; and no wonder, for the descriptions of the latter are often such as to excite dread rather than filial love and reverence. It would not, therefore, be a stretch of the truth to say that Cautiousness, rather than Conscientiousness and Veneration, is the basis of the piety of many, which is simply heathenish. Fear builds their altar; Fear offers the sacrifice.

into a smile, and their influence is not less powerful with its growing years. A mother who is sensible of this will never indulge in a discontented, repining tone, whatever may be the vexations she may have to encounter; neither bodily nor mental suffering will lead her into peevishness or fretfulness. She will teach her children by her own example to look on the bright side of everything, to feel, whatever may happen, that

> "The darkest day,
> Live till to-morrow, will have passed away."

She will show them how to find some good, even in that which at first appears vexatious and disagreeable, and that apparent misfortune often proves to be quite the reverse. If it be a misfortune, still she will lead them to make the best of it. If they are disappointed of one pleasure, she will point out to them those that are still within reach, and that all is not lost because the desired object is unattainable.

The anticipations of children with regard to future pleasure are apt far to exceed the reality, and we ought to make allowance for them, and sympathize with them, not make our cool and experienced feelings the measure of theirs, nor expect them to estimate the value of their anticipated enjoyment by our standard; but if these longings for happiness in store leave the mind restless and disinclined to present duties, they are hurtful and should be checked. A child will soon perceive that pleasure is increased by the consciousness of having omitted nothing that is right to be done, for its sake.

If excessive anticipations of good be injurious, the habit of anticipating evil is much worse. This should never be indulged in by young or old. Many of the dreaded evils never come to pass. Let us not throw away present blessings in fears for the future, but let us take every means in our power to avert the threatened ill, and then leave the success of our efforts to wiser disposal than ours.

Hope is essential to perseverance. If a child, after making one or two ineffectual efforts to accomplish something which he ought to do, or which it is desirable he should do, gives up the attempt despondingly, and says, "I am sure I never can do it," we should not only urge upon him the juvenile lesson, "Try Again," but we should assist him to find out the best way of overcoming the difficulty, and even half do the task with him ourselves, rather than allow him to give up. The pleasure of having surmounted one difficulty will stimulate him to the encounter of another.

It is a general idea that there are times and seasons when we ought not to be cheerful; when our feelings ought to assume a saddened hue, and when we should rather encourage the feeling of gloom than endeavor to dissipate. Perhaps there is truer wisdom in opening as soon as possible the mind in affliction, not only to religious sources of consolation, but to the influence of all alleviating circumstances. A great philosopher and good man used to say, that by long habit he had brought his mind to look upon present trouble as he knew it would appear to him afterward. If we can realize this; if in sorrow we can reckon the comforts that we have left and consider the multitudes who are happy with even less; if we are thankful to God for what remains, and console ourselves with the reflection that if time can not replace our loss, yet every day and every hour will tend to reconcile us to it; if we endeavor to enter at once into the state of mind which a week, a month, a year will bring; then we shall be ready to profit by the lesson of cheerfulness which all Nature joins with the Apostle Paul in giving—"Rejoice always." *

---

* The difference in the mental condition of persons, one of whom is strong and the other weak in the development of this faculty, is as wide as that existing between riches and poverty, or happiness and misery. The politician who works a year in a campaign and is beaten in the election, if he have large Hope, will say: "Never mind, we will win the next election, four years hence." The farmer whose crop fails, will expect from the resting land a double crop the next year. Some are desponding, others gather fresh hope from defeat, and manage, in feeling, to keep on the the crest of the wave.

The owner, who was informed that one of his sheep had given birth to three lambs, instantly anticipated much profit by exhibiting them at the next autumn fair. "But one of the lambs is dead." "All right; then the other two will fare all the better. "But two of them are dead." "Ah! then she can do first-rate by the other." "But all the lambs are dead." "All right, then the sheep will get fat and be ready for an early market." "Yes, father, but the old sheep is dead too." "Is that so? Well, she was a poor thing anyway, and would not have amounted to much if she had lived."

"Hope springs eternal in the human breast,
Man never *is*, but always *to be* blest."

Hope is at least an ingredient in the desire for and expectation of a future state. "It lifts the curtain of time and points to immortality."

WONDER

(OR SPIRITUALITY).

Wonder expresses the superlative degree of the function of this faculty; the feeling usually connected with it is simple Faith or Belief. The world, as we conceive of it, is created in our own minds by our own mental faculties, and the sense of its reality is the result of this feeling. Certain impressions made upon the senses produce within us certain sensations to which we give names as to objects without ourselves, and we believe in their existence as represented by the mind. Mill truly says: "That we know nothing of objects, but the sensations we have from them;" and Hume says: "We may observe that it is universally allowed by philosophers, and is besides pretty obvious of itself, that nothing is ever really present with the mind but its perceptions or impressions and ideas, and that external objects become known to us only by the perceptions which they occasion. Now, since nothing is ever present to the mind but perceptions, and since all ideas are derived from something antecedent to the mind, it follows that it is impossible for us so much as to conceive or form an idea of anything specifically different from ideas and impressions. Let us fix our ideas outside of ourselves as much as possible; let us chase our imaginations to the heavens, or to the utmost limit of the universe; we never really advance a step beyond ourselves, nor can perceive any kind of existence but those perceptions which have appeared in that narrow compass."

Elsewhere, in writing of this faculty, we observed, " The intellectual faculties give ideas, each after its own peculiar mode or form of intelligence; but the *practical belief* attending the action of such faculties is altogether a different thing. Without such a sentiment, ideas would pass over the mind like images over the surface of a mirror, reason would be paralyzed, and we should act like the brutes, only when impelled by instinct, and not from faith. The excess of Hope produces immoderate expectations of felicity not founded on reason; and the excess of Wonder, that is, of this faculty of Faith, produces credulity. The pleasure and wonder expressed by children and adults who have a considerable development of this faculty, at the relation of marvelous stories, miraculous and improbable fictions, proceed from their extra power of belief, from their giving to such tales a reality in their own minds which to others they do not assume." Dr. Thomas Brown has shown that what we call Cause and Effect are mere Antecedence and Consequence, and that there is no reason that we can discover why any one cause should produce any one effect more than another, except that it always has done so—that is, the antecedence and consequence have been observed to be invariable, the belief of a *necessary* connection between cause and effect is produced by this faculty. It results from this that one thing is not more wonderful to young children than another; they believe all things with equal facility. There is no real reason that we know of why one thing should follow another in the relation of cause and effect, except that it does follow it, and there is equally no real reason why one thing should not follow another, however absurd the expectation that it will do so may appear to our mature experience; consequently, chil-

THOMAS WHITAKER.

WONDER—SPIRITUALITY.

PLATE XX.

dren believe equally in all things—in the most monstrous prodigies of romance as well as in the most simple and common events, until experience or their teacher has given a proper direction to their faith, and taught them the difference between accidental and invariable antecedence. Neither is this kind of faith peculiar to childhood: almost every one's religious creed contains mysteries, frequently contradictions, which are believed equally with the simplest articles of faith. Children easily believe—they have to be taught to disbelieve. They personify everything, and live in a world of their own creating, which is as real to them as our world is to us. Anything, from a cushion to a boot-jack, makes into a doll, and the doll is a living person—animals talk, trees hold council, and flowers have affections. The extreme eagerness with which children listen to "a tale," particularly if it relates to the wonderful, points this faculty out as a most valuable vehicle for instruction, and for the exercise of our best feelings. While all the faculties of the mind are bent with earnest attention upon the story, they are open to receive the lessons it may convey, and the vivid association of interest will stamp them lastingly upon the memory. No accomplishment is more useful to a mother or teacher than a facility in the power of throwing instruction into the shape of a tale; if this be not naturally possessed, it will become easy by practice. It does not follow that every tale we tell to children must have a moral, and we should be sorry to banish all the old nursery tales which have been the delight of many and many a generation, although entirely unincumbered with any moral, except those that offend against right principle and good taste. The introduction of supernatural horrors to children's minds has been already deprecated, as far as can now be necessary.

The proper use of this faculty, and the direction we should endeavor to give to it in our children, is faith in ourselves, and in those upon whom their guardianship depends: faith whose fruit is confidence and obedience. In childhood all is mystery, doubt, and ignorance; let the child, then, lean upon its parent with that trust which produces hope and love. And if a child be properly trained, the feeling in mature age will be readily transferred from the earthly to the Heavenly Father. Ignorance and Mystery must still exist, but there can be no Doubt. God has planted within us moral instincts, affording a natural revelation of His Will, and their dictates must not be disregarded in obedience to what fallible man may proclaim as another revelation. Those in whom such faculties are fully developed, and and who have received otherwise a good education, must believe that God wills the good of His creatures; that if He punishes them it is for their good; that they have but to learn His Will and do it, to secure their happiness and well-being; that on all occasions having done what He commands, we may safely leave the result to Him; that He knows on all occasions what is best for all, and that we may safely, therefore, place ourselves with all confidence in His hands; that evil and all things will be made to work together for good, and to prepare the way for the reign of the true and the beautiful even upon this earth.*

---

* Faith, belief, hunger for the strange, unusual and wonderful, seem to arise from this faculty. The human soul

The feelings of which we have now to treat, are good or bad according to the other feelings with which they ally themselves. They may be equally the servants of all the faculties: thus Attention, Perseverance, Firmness, Imitation, may belong equally to the murderer and to the philanthropist. They are not virtues in themselves, but they give concentration, power, and permanence to the other faculties.

---

yearns after something real beside real estate, something true beside mathematics, something enduring beside granite and diamonds. It is an element in discovery or invention, at least tends to inspire the feeling of wonderful possibilities in the realm of the undiscovered. One having little of this faculty and of Ideality will suppose present development covers all that is possible, and he will not believe in nor look for more. Hence it is that inventors are sometimes impractical dreamers, and believe in much more than they have the talent to develop. Hence "perpetual motion" is always being sought for and confidently expected, by some. The navigation of the air has its devotees, but most thinkers see obstacles which they feel sure are insurmountable. Religious faith seems to be rich, full, and comforting, in proportion to the development of this faculty. Conscientiousness and Benevolence are sometimes strong in those who lack Veneration and Spirituality. They are just and kind, but they are called skeptics, and sometimes infidels. Some we find who have Spirituality large and Veneration moderate, and they see little significance in worship, but they have an upreach of soul which carries them beyond the dust and din of secular life, and gives them that high communion which is unutterable.

CONCENTRATIVENESS AND INHABITIVENESS.*

Man is the creature of habit; most of his actions are not the result of volition, but of habit; and the great object of the training of the feelings is to produce virtuous habits, for these alone can be relied upon; with them only is "the soul's calm sunshine." Much of the exercise which the mind is required to go through is valuable from no other result but the formation of habit. If nothing else follows from order and system and application, we ought to be satisfied with that.

---

* Mr. Combe recognized an organ located above Philoprogenitiveness and below Self-Esteem, and called it Concentrativeness. Dr. Spurzheim called the same region Inhabitiveness, and between them both they described both functions, viz.: union and continuity of thought, and the sense of local habitation. American Phrenologists recognize and describe both faculties, and ascribe the lower part of the region in question to the faculty of Love of Home, or Inhabitiveness, and the upper, to Concentrativeness or Continuity.

Those who have the upper part of the space in question large, manifest unity of thought and feeling, patient, plodding persistency. When it is small, persons fly from one thing to another; are adapted to rapidly changing conditions and avocations, dislike prolixity in statement, or permanency in the processes of business; they like many things to look after, attend to particulars, and do well in retail or variety business; can superintend factories where many things and processes are to be attended to in quick succession. One having it large plods; prefers a long, straight, level road, a long seam, or steady and changeless job; a solid page or column in reading; and they are likely to be prolix as writers, speakers, or talkers. By observation

R. MURCHISON.

CONTINUITY—CONCENTRATIVENESS.

PLATE XXI.

Habits of industry, of attention, of self-subjection, of self-denial, are more valuable than intellectual acquirements, and how we learn is of more consequence in childhood than how much we learn. The continual dropping of water will wear away the hardest stone, and attention and perseverance will overcome the greatest difficulties. The object of the above faculties seems to be to aid in forming habits. Much has been written by mental philosophers upon the power of association, and perhaps the importance of the subject has not been overrated. Concentrativeness gives the desire to retain emotions and ideas, and instinctive love of dwelling upon them when present, until an asso-

among vocations we find that both characters are required —one can bend over the accounts; the other looks after customers, and the great variety of articles to be judged of, described and sold.

INHABITIVENESS.

That a faculty exists which lies at the foundation of patriotism, love of country and home, there can be no room for doubt, nor does it seem so much to partake of merely fixedness or concentrativeness to place, as to give pleasure and pride, nay joy, at the possession and ownership of a place of abode. How we adorn and decorate! What hallowed memories cluster around it! The cat shows fondness for home and permits its last and only human friends to leave it while she remains in the home and risks the reception the new comers may give her. The dog, on the contrary, loving home, no doubt, but loving friends better, will whine his regret at leaving the only home he knows, but he will sacrifice a home so often as his master chooses to move, and cling, through Adhesiveness or Friendship to the people, and leave the home behind.

ciation is formed between certain feelings, and also between such feelings and particular intellectual states. Inhabitiveness dwells with as much satisfaction upon places as Concentrativeness does upon states of mind, producing attachment to home and the love of country.

Upon Concentrativeness mainly depends the "power of Attention," which has been so deservedly dwelt upon by writers on education, as indispensable to the culture of the intellect, and also of the moral nature; for, without it, the efforts of the instructor would be like making a rope of sand. It is probably less frequently deficient than is imagined; for the attention of the mind to its internal ideas is often the cause of the apparent inattention to those presented from without. Its right direction depends upon the development of the superior faculties; and if they be weak, the lower ones will seize possession of this stronghold and occupy it for their own ends. Where this is not the case, and the higher powers hold their rightful supremacy, one of them may predominate over the rest so much as to fix the attention of the mind to the exclusion of others more seasonable; it should be the endeavor of the teacher to ascertain this leading faculty, and to counteract its undue predominance by exciting the others. The direction of this disposition will, therefore, depend upon the prevailing feeling, unless checked by the moral sense which teaches that it is right to give the whole mind to the present duty.

If, for instance, a child who has an inordinate love of eating be receiving a lesson, an incidental allusion in the course of it to the beloved subject may fill his mind with ideas of good things in reversion; the same lesson

WM. M. EVARTS.
INHABITIVENESS.

PLATE XXII.

may, from another association, induce a second roaming in imagination through the fields and woods; a third, to revel in the regions of romance—while the instructor marvels that his useful lesson makes so little impression. And all this with no deficiency, but merely a misdirection of the feeling of which we are speaking. A child of four years and a-half old, whose teacher had tried to explain to him the necessity of self-control on this point, showed that he was not too young to understand it. The next time he was occupied with his lesson, his favorite playmate entered the room; in a tone of command he addressed himself, "*Me* don't look up when Annie comes."

Where there is no original want of this feeling it is often much weakened by injudicious management in infancy, as many excellent writers have observed. The active, impatient nurse will not suffer the child's attention to attach itself undisturbed to the object which takes its fancy. When he grasps the new substance, fixes his eyes intently upon it, begins to consider what it is like and what it is for, she snatches it hastily away and attracts his notice to something else : thus preventing the little philosopher from making his own experiments and drawing his own deductions. By a constant repetition of this treatment, the mind becomes incapacitated for patient and continued thought.

"We must remember, also, that many children," says Richter, "have, in common with men, an incapability of instantaneous cessation from what they are doing. Often no threatening can stop their laughter. We should remember the converse when they are crying, in order to treat their weakness as a physician rather than as a judge."

If, on the contrary, this faculty be constitutionally weak, we must be careful to make the subjects upon which it is exercised as interesting as possible, in order that the pain of giving attention may be outweighed by the pleasure it will occasion. A celebrated author well remarks, " There is no memory without attention, and no attention without interest."

Perhaps the excess of this faculty is less common than its absence, but this excess has sometimes to be corrected. It is possible to pay too much attention to a study or pursuit, excellent and important in itself, and to suffer the mind to be engrossed by it to the exclusion of more extended and general information, until we become partial and contracted in our views, and incapable of estimating the true value of our own department of knowledge.

We may sometimes trace the prevalence of the feeling, in a minor degree, in the tenacity with which some persons cling to a subject in conversation, and the pain which they appear to feel when compelled to turn their attention to something else.

When a child seems absorbed so much in one particular mental occupation as to take no interest in anything else, it is desirable that he should be shown how all the branches of knowledge are connected with and throw light upon each other, and how he can not even know all relating to his favorite subject without enlarging his acquirements.

It occasionally happens that a child appears to be haunted by a particular set of feelings and ideas; they follow him through the day and form his dreams by night. This, perhaps, is owing to some morbid state of the system, as well as to an excess of Concentrativeness; but in either case the mind should be gently led away to opposite ideas, and both mind and body receive as much relaxation as possible.

FIRMNESS.

Firmness gives strength and efficiency to every virtue and quality of mind. Constancy, fortitude, determination, perseverance, which are its manifestations, are essential to force of character and consistency in action. The character may be amiable, the wish to do good sincere, but without unity of purpose and perseverance in execution, even virtuous efforts will produce small fruits. The Apostle says: "He that wavereth is like a wave of the sea, driven with the wind and tossed." We have more cause to fear the want of the feeling than its predominance, for what in childhood may show itself in stubbornness and obstinacy, will, if the proper cultivation of all the other faculties be attended to, be displayed in manhood in the virtues of perseverance, fortitude, and patience.

A child who is deficient in Firmness will be prone to yield to the impulses of any feeling that may predominate at the moment; he will be apt to procrastinate, to shrink from doing anything disagreeable, however necessary. If a tooth must be drawn, or a bitter medicine taken, or a tedious sum worked again, the evil moment is put off if possible. Undertakings will be continually begun and continually thrown aside, uncompleted, in favor of new schemes. Good resolutions, formed when the mind is fresh and active, will give way when the stimulus is withdrawn, or when temptation presents itself.

Where this weakness is observed, the force of habit must be brought to bear against it. Regular and constant application must be enforced, and kept up by the assistance of the best feelings; but only for short and certain periods. No disinclination, no idle excuse, must be permitted to postpone the performance of a present duty. The pleasure of conquest over self in submitting to a present pain, and thus avoiding a future greater one, besides all the pains of irresolution, must be made clear and enhanced; and whenever any degree of self-conquest or perseverance is shown, it should be encouraged by sympathy and assistance.

If it happen that the feeling of Firmness is stronger than the intellect, it will take the form of obstinacy, because, in that case, the judgment is not always capable of determining when Firmness is misplaced. This frequently occurs, and very delicate management is required to prevent occasional obstinacy from settling down into a habit of perverseness. Some parents and teachers have themselves the love of authority so strong, that they would actually prefer that a child should do right because they command it than of its own accord; it requires a stretch of magnanimity of which all are not capable, to be satisfied that their child should judge and act wisely without interference on their part. Their aim seems to be less that of teaching a child to walk alone, than to strengthen the leading strings which attach it to themselves. But let them remember that they thus gratify their own propensities at the child's

MARSHALL P. WILDER.

FIRMNESS.

PLATE XXIII.

expense. It is a common notion that the first thing to be done in training a child is to "break its will." Are parents sure that this does not arise from the love of power in themselves? Little do they imagine the evils generated in the harsh process!

There are few children who would not obey from motives of affection and duty, if they were made to feel that nothing was required of them but what was right and reasonable. Implicit obedience should rarely be enforced, unless the confidence and affection on the part of the child be strong enough to counteract the violence that such a requirement must do to his feelings. Of course this does not refer to very early childhood, when obedience must frequently be required without rendering a reason, plainly because the reasoning power is not developed to receive it; but even then the command itself must be reasonable.

The word obstinacy is often applied to the conduct of children, when in reality very different feelings come into play, all producing similar external manifestations. A child may be directed to do something which he thinks involves an injury to himself; his natural Firmness will assist the feeling of Oppositiveness in resisting the command; it may include something which he imagines to be wrong; his Firmness will then be supported by his sense of right; or he may not really understand what the injunction means; or may oppose it from the mere superabundance of Firmness itself; which last alone is obstinacy, strictly speaking. Now, all these cases we are apt to call cases of obstinacy, and treat them in the same manner, whereas they proceed from totally different sources, and require dealing with accordingly. In the last instance we must be sure that the command is *necessary* before it is given, and kindness must unite with determination in exacting obedience. But all occasion for combats of this description should be studiously avoided; it would be much wiser to give too few commands than to give too many.*

---

* There are two kinds of Firmness, or two phases of the manifestation, apparently irrespective of the temperament of the constitution, and the development of the other mental organs. The first is persistence; the tendency to hold on quietly and wait for a chance. The man who manages the hawser which has been thrown over the post on the dock, and has been passed around the cleet on the ship's deck, waits for the surging waters or the easy rolling of the ship to bring it up toward the dock, and thus " slack the line," when he expertly loosens from the cleet and " hauls in the slack; " but as soon as the vessel begins to "fall off" again he "makes fast" to the cleet, and thus he manages until the vessel is brought up and securely fastened to the dock. Men quietly hold on their way; if met by bold opposition they may not meet it by strife, but wait for opening circumstances, when they make progress again.

The other kind of Firmness is called obstinacy. It tries to force things. It will not wait; becomes impatient, and frets and worries if hindered or compelled to change a course. Two brothers quarreled about the division of the homestead farm, and lived thirty years near neighbors without speaking to each other. One of them being, as he thought, near his death, sent for his brother and said he wished to make peace before he died, which was agreed to. A few days afterward the sick man had so far improved as to hope for recovery, and told the visiting brother he thought he might possibly recover. He replied, "If you die all our matters are settled, but remember, if you get well the old grudge holds good."

There is a passage in a recent magazine article containing some excellent remarks touching this subject, although it does not bear exactly upon the feeling under notice, as the obstinacy which proceeds from resistance to a supposed injury is, as above said, not a case of the genuine feeling: "Nothing fosters obstinacy like contention. It has been said, and there may be some truth in the idea, that it is right to do battle once with an obstinate child, and by overcoming it make him aware of his habit, and also convince him of his power and yours to conquer it. But it is very questionable whether these victories do not leave behind them a resentfulness and soreness which it takes years to efface. However this may be with regard to habits already formed, certain it is that one should try to prevent the formation of the habit, a thing only to be done by analyzing the feeling. What is obstinacy but the resistance to a supposed injury? Is there any other cure for it than a conviction in the child of the lovingness and good sense of its conductor? Is that conviction likely to be wrought by the tortures by which people usually seek to conquer a fit of obstinacy? Would obstinacy ever spring up under an intelligent guidance? Must it not have been engendered by a loss of confidence, caused by a quantity of useless requisitions on the part of the educator? Here comes in that principle of action which meets us at every turn, viz., to wait patiently till experience shall have tutored the will. No one will obstinately resist that which he sees to be his good; it is for this seeing that the parent must so often be content to wait. Too great care can not be taken, likewise, that we do not call that obstinacy which is often stupidity

on the one hand, or firmness of principle on the other."
"To be very careful not to tax a child unjustly with obstinacy, or to engender it by ill-advised demands, and to be content when it exists to let it melt away gradually under the influence of growing affection and sympathy; such should be the course adopted toward the obstinate. Nor should one ever lose sight of the fact that all wrong is but excess of good, and that that which under the name of obstinacy looks so hideous, springs from the very principle of our nature, which, well directed, we should all venerate under a thousand lovely forms, such as firmness, fortitude, liberty, decision, etc."

Again, therefore, we say, avoid, if possible, doing battle with obstinacy; to resist the feeling only strengthens it. Employ patience, kindness, reasoning; threats and punishment only increase the evil. Of course there are times and occasions when commands must be given, and when this is the case, they must be obeyed *always*, and *under all circumstances;* but such instances should be very rare.

No eminence is ever reached without continued effort; nothing valuable is ever attained without perseverance; let us, therefore, carefully cultivate this faculty. Endure hardness, says the preacher—and a large proportion of that which is disagreeable must enter into our every-day life; this faculty will mainly help us to bear it, will put us in harmony with it, and even furnish a kind of pleasure of its own in the fortitude and endurance called for:

"Into life's goblet freely press
The leaves that give it bitterness."

To do only that which is pleasant, soon engenders a

state of mind altogether at variance with steady application and continued effort; it makes self-sacrifice hard, and duty difficult. Self-denial must be practised on small as well as on great occasions, and those whose habits are self-indulgent will be weak, irresolute, and easily overcome by temptation.

As a gladiator trained the body, so must we train the mind to self-sacrifice "to endure all things," to meet and overcome difficulty and danger. We must take the rough and thorny road as well as the smooth and pleasant; and a portion, at least, of our daily duty must be hard and disagreeable; for the mind can not be kept strong and healthy in perpetual sunshine only, and the most dangerous of all states is that of constantly recurring pleasure, ease, and prosperity. Most persons will find difficulties and hardships enough without seeking them; let them not repine, but take them as a part of that educational discipline necessary to fit the mind to arrive at its highest good.

IMITATION.

The natural language of every feeling is more or less marked on the person and in the countenance, and no doubt there is a faculty which at once recognizes and sympathizes with this natural language of the feelings. Through this unknown faculty we gain an instinctive knowledge of character, as through it we enter at once into the mind of another, and for a time may be almost said to become a part of that other mind.* From its unusual development in such men as Bacon, Shakespeare, and Scott, is probably owing their deep insight into human nature. Many phrenologists now admit its existence. As this instinct induces sympathy of feeling, so Imitation produces sympathy of action, and copies the manners and gestures of others. Every spirituality or idea, before it can be born into the world, and become manifestible to others, must take some

---

* The organ which, in America, is known as "Human Nature," located above Comparison, enables us to appreciate strangers, to like one and dislike another at first sight, without being conscious of any reason for it which we can frame into words.

The old story of Dr. Fell, who had a pupil in his school between whom and himself there seemed to be a natural antagonism, illustrates this faculty. Just before recess the boy had been busy writing something on his slate, and turned it over as he went out. The doctor, perhaps unconsciously to himself, was watching to find occasion of complaint against the boy, inquisitively turned over the slate and read the lines—

> "I do not like you, Dr. Fell,
> The reason why I can not tell;
> But this one thing I know full well,
> I do *not* like you, Dr Fell."

This set the doctor thinking, and like a wise man, he tried by a course of justice and confidence to overcome the mutual repugnance. If we begin to manifest kindness toward one we do not like, we soon conquer our unkind spirit; partly, perhaps, because by kindness we call out a kindlier spirit from the other toward ourselves; but chiefly because the exercise in ourselves of the feelings of justice and kindness brings us into a happy and self-approving state of mind.

GEN'L JOHN GLOVER.
IMITATION.

PLATE XXIV

bodily or material form. Imitation copies only that material form, and where the feeling is strong it is sometimes very difficult to distinguish the mere imitation of an idea or feeling from the genuine feeling itself.

Imitation has a very powerful effect in forming and fashioning our minds and habits. It is owing to this feeling, added to the force of sympathy and association, already spoken of, that, imperceptibly to ourselves, we take the direction of our feelings and the tone of mind and manners from the age and society to which we belong, and it is not without a strong effort that we can break through the spell which binds us to think, to feel, and to act with all around us. It is intended to make the members of the social body more harmonious. It influences us equally in less important concerns; our gestures, our modes of speech, our habits of life, the regulation of our mutual intercourse, our dress—all follow the models which the fashion of society sets before us. Owing to this copying propensity, each nation has its peculiar characteristics; the European and the Chinese have each different degrees only of the same mental faculties; but, so great is the diversity in their external habits, that we might readily believe them to belong to separate planets.

Boerhaave relates "that a schoolmaster near Leyden being squint-eyed, it was found that the children placed under his care soon exhibited a like obliquity of vision."

This faculty seems to be given as the great help in education, but it is a help which throws an immense responsibility upon parents and teachers. The vices and evil habits of parents descend by its means from generation to generation—but, through the same means, none of their excellencies can be wholly lost. Thus a good system of education may do much when aided by a good example, but nothing whatever without it. Powerful as is the operation of this feeling, and therefore of example, we must be careful lest children do, from the mere imitation of those with whom they associate, what ought to proceed from a better feeling—from a higher principle. They who are not in the habit of looking minutely into motives, frequently mistake the instinctive action of this feeling for one originating in a higher source. This is a dangerous error, for where imitation alone is the source of good conduct, that good conduct obviously has no root in itself, and will cease as soon as the example is withdrawn. The influence of example, therefore, in order to be a safe, must be a silent one. We must be careful never to say to children, Do so and so because your parents and instructors, those whom you respect and love, do so; but because it is right, it is kind, it is wise. While we gather around children not only circumstances, but persons who will contribute to mould their characters, their manners, and their habits to the standard we approve, we must sparingly, if at all, present them as models; for besides, as there are imperfections even among the excellent of the earth, a child will probably imitate the errors which are associated with the virtues—the mind will also be led to be satisfied with referring to an outward tribunal of right, rather than to the inner one of duty. To place the companions and equals of children before them as examples, is more dangerous still, from the risk of exciting envy and jealousy instead of the wish to emulate.

At the same time that we aim at opening the mind to receive all the good which radiates from the examples around, we must infuse it into a principle, which shall enable it to repel the emanations of evil which are also widely diffused. Singularity is to be avoided if it can be consistently with reason and justice; but when it can not, then it becomes us to resist the promptings of the feeling which impels us to do as others do—to dare to be singular when the world is wrong; and when we become cognizant of the actual requirements of true humanity in its full development, the amount of time, wealth, and happiness—of the good, true, and beautiful, now sacrificed in the world of fashion—we shall see that it is no small part of the instructor's duty to give this faculty a wise direction, and to check its instinctive manifestation.

There are many obvious abuses against which we shall have to guard in the education of such a propensity. The habit of indiscriminate mimicry tends above all things to the depression of veneration, and worse than this, Imitation is capable of becoming a powerful ally of love of approbation, in seeming to be virtuous instead of really being so.

THE FEELING OF THE LUDICROUS,

OR MIRTHFULNESS.

Man has been defined as "a laughing animal," and his dignity need not reject the definition, for it would scarcely compensate him for the loss of the characteristic. When the progress of years and the cares of life have somewhat sobered the spirits, who does not look back with regret to the joyous mirth of his childhood, and if he can not return to those happy days when he himself was "tickled by a straw," delight in the hearty merriment of those with whom they are not past? One of the happy effects of the mixture of all ages in society, is the enlivening influence of the light-heartedness and gayety of those in whom life is young, upon those whose animal spirits are no longer as buoyant as theirs.*

"Laughing is good for digestion," as the old saw hath it, and "he that is of a merry heart hath a continual feast," but "there is a season for all things under the heaven." In very young children laughter is little

---

* Mirthfulness, the power to appreciate the ludicrous, is especially a human faculty. Of this the lower animals are denied. No doubt wit, or a sense of the ridiculous and absurd, is a great aid to the reason, since Causality and Comparison perceive the congruous and appropriate, Mirthfulness enables us to perceive the incongruous and absurd, and awakens a desire to laugh. Anything absurd must be untrue, and wit is a kind of negative touchstone of truth. True wit is not confined to the age of youth. There is in youth an exuberance of the tendency to laugh; almost anything to which they are not accustomed awakens the desire to laugh. But when the mind becomes ripened by time and culture, real wit sparkles in the mind of the healthy person of fifty, with brilliancy and intensity equal to anything experienced in earlier life. It may not make so much noise, neither does a stream after it has become larger and worn a deeper channel.

ALLEN GRIFFITH.
MIRTHFULNESS.
PLATE XXV.

more than the expression of a sudden feeling of happiness; in time it becomes, in addition, the outward sign of the sense of the ludicrous, which often shows itself to a degree which demands restraint; they know how to deprecate its effects who have tried time after time to gain a child's serious attention for five minutes, but have failed as often, on account of their pupil's finding at every turn something that excites this feeling. When this happens, the teacher must studiously avoid any word, tone, or look, which can awaken a ludicrous association, and pass over without the least notice the child's attempts to break into witticism, until the work requiring attention shall be concluded. Another method was tried with a child whose mirthful mood was quite incompatible with attention to his lesson—he *could not help* laughing, he said. He was advised to jump up, run into a corner of the room, and laugh as hard as he could. He very readily obeyed, and ran laughing to his post, followed by his adviser, who, laughing herself, exhorted him to persevere: "Oh that is not half long enough; try again." He did his best, but a few minutes were enough to bring him to his sober senses, and he returned to his lesson quite cured of his risibility.

There may be a strong sense of the ludicrous without the power of exciting it in others, which last is wit, and depends upon the combination of this sense with other mental faculties and peculiarities. In proportion to the degree of intellectual cultivation which accompanies it, will the pleasure it gives be more or less exquisite. Children, therefore, can seldom enjoy the higher species of wit, because their knowledge is too limited to enable them to understand it; but whenever they can, they are quick to appreciate it. They are generally, however, most pleased with humor, drollery, play upon words, and the inferior kinds of wit which depend upon the power of imitation, and their own efforts at wit are for the most part of this class. The sayings of children may be accidentally witty to those who can perceive an incongruity or an unexpected relation which is quite hidden to the children themselves. The laughter thus excited will abash a child of a timid disposition, and add to its natural reserve, while another of a different nature will be emboldened by it to the utterance of fresh conceits, or perhaps to the repetition of the same, over and over again, not doubting that the same effect of surprise and laughter will follow as at the first. When we laugh at such things, we should explain to children why we do so, and not leave them with a vague impression on their minds that they have said something wrong, or very clever. The remarks of an intelligent child of quick perception often contain, unconsciously to himself, the elements of wit. When the child, Charles Lamb, asked his sister in the churchyard, after reading the epitaphs on the tombstones which memorialized the virtues of each of the departed underneath, "And where do the *naughty* people lie?" he did not know that there was wit in the inquiry.

There is so great a charm in the sportive play of fancy and wit, that there is no danger of their being neglected and undervalued, or that the native talent for them will remain undeveloped; our chief solicitude must be to keep them, even in their wildest flight, still in subjection to duty and benevolence. We must not allow ourselves to be betrayed into an approving smile at any effusions of wit and humor which are tinctured in the slightest degree by ill-nature. A child will watch the expression of our countenance to see how far he may venture, and if he find that he has the power to amuse us in spite of ourselves, we have no longer any hold over him from respect, and he will go rioting on in his sallies until he is tired, and seek at every future opportunity to renew his triumph. Wit undirected by benevolence generally falls into personal satire—the keenest instrument of unkindness; it is so easy to laugh at the expense of our friends and neighbors—they furnish such ready materials for our wit, that all the moral forces require to be arrayed against the propensity, and its earliest indications checked. We may satirize error, but we must compassionate the erring, and this we must always teach by example to children, not only in what we say of others before them, but in our treatment of themselves. We should never use ridicule toward them, except when it is so evidently good-natured that its spirit can not be mistaken; the agony which a sensitive child feels on being held up before others as an object of ridicule, even for a trifling error, a mistake, or a peculiarity, is not soon forgotten, nor easily forgiven. When we wish, therefore, to excite contrition for a serious fault, ridicule should never be employed, as the feelings it raises are directly opposed to self-reproach.

The love of the ridiculous often becomes so excessive, that the mind is incapable of the effort of being serious for long together, even upon the most serious subjects. It is continually darting off in search of the ludicrous and the absurd, and the associations thus formed are most detrimental to the progress of mental and moral improvement. A peculiar gesture, the disarrangement of a collar or a cravat, the mis-pronunciation of a word, are enough to mar the effect of the most instructive and eloquent discourse. We attempt to reason, and are met by a jest, a pun, a quibble. To turn everything into ridicule is as profitless as it is wearisome. But wit should sparkle among the solid endowments of the mind that is fully competent to educate—there should be the power of amusing as well as that of instructing. The influence which a playful wit has over children, is shown by the preference which they display at a very early age toward persons who possess it, and that which it exerts not only over them, but over all whose minds are able to appreciate it, proves it to be, when instructed by the intellect, elevated and refined by ideality, and warmed by benevolence, one of the choicest gifts to man which Nature has bestowed.

Such are the feelings which by phrenologists are termed *established*, and although the list can by no means be considered complete, yet all must admit that it contains the principal elements of our mental nature. Some of the feelings, as they are now delineated in the works of phrenologists, are no doubt too complex in their function, and will be resolved, as the science advances, into more simple elements; but still, as the uses and properties of atmospheric air were the same before it was found to consist of oxygen and nitrogen as after, so any future division or sub-division of the mental faculties will not falsify our present deductions concerning their uses and properties which we have obtained from a consideration of them in the aggregate. It is also beyond a doubt that there are some primitive feelings which are not included in the above list; but enough is not yet known of them to speak decidedly of their education; such are the Love of Knowledge, the Love of the Past, Mental Imitation, etc. As there is a love or desire of property, so also is there a desire for mental acquirement—a love of knowledge for its own sake; and a certain diversity in the mode in which persons mentally connect themselves with the events of life—some always living in the past, never in the present or the future—others never looking back, always forward—point to some elemental difference for which the faculties we have named are not sufficient to account. So, also, there is doubtless an intuition into character—a faculty which reads the natural language of the mental states, and which was possessed in a superior degree by such men as Shakespeare, Lord Bacon, and Sir Walter Scott. But incomplete and imperfect as the phrenological classification of the feelings may be, yet, being true as far as it goes, the exposition of the principles of our nature which it furnishes is invaluable in education. To give the use of each faculty, point out the abuse of which it is susceptible, and show in what that abuse consists, must greatly aid a judicious person practically acquainted with the management of children, and in the habit of applying principles to practice. By the assistance of a clever, practical phrenologist, or by close attention to natural disposition, the proportion in which each feeling is possessed may be ascertained, and tolerably correct data obtained on which to form our system for the restraint of some feelings and the strengthening of others. It must be admitted that the faculties seldom act alone, but usually in combination with others, and some qualities of mind are of so complex a character that they could not properly be included under any of the separate heads; but, still, if each feeling be trained aright, the virtue which is the compound result will be certain to show itself in full strength.

The following subjects could not be properly treated under the same headings as any of the mental faculties taken separately: Authority and Obedience, Temper, Punishment, Manners, Example:

AUTHORITY AND OBEDIENCE.

It is desirable to leave a child as much at liberty as circumstances will conveniently admit, and to give as few commands and prohibitions as possible. Let the child's limbs and affections have full play and free scope, and let our endeavor be to assist the natural growth and enter fully into his mind and spirit. But if a command *must* be given, give it at once, as that from which there can be no appeal; the reasons for it are better given afterward, when there can be no interested motives to prevent the child from seeing them in their proper light. Obedience must always be enforced. The penalty of disobedience must be as certain as the pain which follows the putting the hand in the fire; for a child must be taught what he will find through life—that there is a law controlling his free will for his own good. As much as possible let a child's conduct be the result of his own free will by a judicious arrangement of circumstances about him, rather than of positive command; for what a child can be led to do of

SAMUEL SLOAN.

AUTHORITY.

PLATE XXVI.

himself is much more valuable in its after result than that which is regulated by another's will. There is much in choosing just the right instant for making a demand; to stop in the midst of any interesting pursuit is always painful. Allow for infirmity of temper, and as much as possible let all feeling subside before commands are given. We may as well command a child not to feel the toothache as not to feel anger and irritation. Never forget what a child must be—that is, what belongs to childhood, and exercise authority as little as possible with regard to those things which a child must necessarily grow out of in a few years.

TEMPER.

Bad temper is oftener the result of unhappy circumstances than of an unhappy organization; it frequently, however, has a physical cause, and a peevish child often needs dieting more than correcting. Some children are more prone to show temper than others, and sometimes on account of qualities which are valuable in themselves. For instance, a child of active temperament, sensitive feeling, and eager purpose, is more likely to meet with constant jars and rubs than a dull, passive child, and if he is of an open nature, his inward irritation is immediately shown in bursts of passion. If you repress these ebullitions by scolding and punishment, you only increase the evil, by changing passion into sulkiness. A cheerful, good-tempered tone of your own, a sympathy with his trouble, whenever the trouble has arisen from no ill-conduct on his part, are the best antidotes; but it would be better still to prevent beforehand, as much as possible, all sources of annoyance.

Never fear spoiling children by making them too happy. Happiness is the atmosphere in which all good affections grow—the wholesome warmth necessary to make the heart-blood circulate healthily and freely; unhappiness the chilling pressure which produces here an inflammation, there an excrescence, and, worst of all, "the mind's green and yellow sickness—ill-temper." Make a child unhappy by continually thwarting him, chiding him, and punishing him, and ten to one he will soon show an evil temper of his own, and a distortion of his moral nature. The friction of trial and disappointment may be very well afterward, when the character has acquired a degree of elasticity and toughness; but in tender childhood it is purely destructive. The trials of childhood do not prepare for the trials of manhood. That man is stronger to endure and overcome whose childhood has been happy and unruffled. A cheerful temper is the best friend we can set out in life with, and we have a heavy charge to bring against our mothers and nurses, if by their petulance and mismanagement they have made us part company. The virtues of self-denial and self-control are better fostered under happy than under unhappy influences; children will delight to make little sacrifices for those they love, if asked to do so in a pleasant tone; and the moral feeling will grow apace under the kindly interchange of good offices between elders and youngers; whereas, the dictatorial manner which those in authority sometimes assume, immediately gathers the frost about the young spirit, and transforms every good feeling into an irresistible desire to be naughty. Bad temper, oftener than we imagine, proceeds from a lurking spirit of revenge

HANS MAKART.

TEMPER.

PLATE XXVII.

for something ugly in our own tone or manner. Fear restrains the child from open resistance or passion; so he takes refuge in sulkiness and a general determination to be disagreeable and perverse. Many persons have a most unfortunate intonation when giving a command, injunction, or reproof—whether to their servants or children—which worse than nullifies all the good they intend. If a mother suspect this defect in herself, we beseech her to ponder over the mischief of letting this association gain strength in herself, and carefully tutor herself till every grain of disagreeableness is excluded from her method of reproving. If a mother be positively ill-tempered, the children have but a poor chance; it is next to impossible that they should not catch a malady so infectious; but only those persons who have much to do with children can know how difficult it is to control the temper at all times, and how important.* Honor be to the governess who makes

---

* It should not be forgotten, that if a mother have an ill-temper, the child has most likely inherited from her no small degree of her spirit. It often happens that a stepmother gets along much more smoothly with the children than their own mother—is practically more kind and just to the children, and that they love her better than they could have loved their own mother if she had been spared; for the simple reason that her disposition may be more amiable; they certainly are not so much alike as they and their real mother, and therefore their sharp points of character do not come in the same places; and therefore they do not mutually annoy each other as the child and its own mother would have done. We believe the average training and treatment of stepmothers toward stepchildren, are quite as good, and much more uniform and successful than is

the daily tasks pleasant and profitable by her cheerful voice and manner, and overcomes the listlessness or fretfulness of her pupils by a happy mixture of briskness and gentleness; when, perhaps, meanwhile her own thoughts are far away, and burdened with many a sad feeling. And also honor to the mother who can bear the noisy overflow of her children's high spirits, when her own are under par, and return gentle answers to their constant, importunate queries, when suffering from bodily weakness or mental anxiety.

PUNISHMENT.

The wholesome administration of punishment demands the most delicate skill and clear-sightedness, with undeviating rectitude of purpose. It is a medicine which, by too frequent use, not only loses all its efficaciousness, but injures and tends to destroy the natural functions of the mind. The mind of a young child in a healthy state—that is, with well-balanced feelings and propensities—is naturally disposed to love goodness and hate wrong-doing, and has a sufficient rectifying power in itself to recover from slight deviations, which is only disturbed and perverted by external interference. If the undue excitement of some selfish inclination has led a child into naughtiness, the aid of the parent may be required by gentle reprimand and the contagion of kindly feeling to restore the bal-

---

the case where the natural tie exists—or it would be so if the relatives of the first wife would mind their own business and not directly or indirectly awaken in the children of the first mother a spirit of jealousy and distrust of the stepmother.

ance of moral perception; but this done, no more is needed; the re-awakened conscience will inflict its salutary pain, aided by the humiliation of honest shame. Whenever these best of guardians perform their part, punishment would be only injurious. The love of goodness is restored—only encouragement in the return to it is required. Let the child feel that its parent only wishes him to be good, and let him feel that as soon as he is good he has a right to be happy. As soon as the naughtiness subsides, and the desire for goodness returns, there should be no fear of punishment to check it; let the affectionate smile be waiting to greet its first appearance, and no grave lecture recall the sullenness that is past. This winning of children out of their infant foibles is quite different from the weak indulgence which spoils them; clogging their stomachs with most deleterious sweets, and destroying their appreciation of healthy food—the bread of life. There can not be too strict vigilance on the part of parents to keep children from the path of wrong, and to draw them from it by unceasing patient efforts, when they have once relapsed. However small the sin—however even *pretty* the naughtiness may appear in its miniature proportions, let parents remember it is great to them; its deadly nature is the same, and will infallibly develop itself in time. Let there be no indulgence here, let their displeasure attend every fault, but let their cordial approbation immediately accompany virtue. So that we should say, as a general rule, let there be *no* punishment—by which we mean the express external infliction of pain, either mentally or bodily—after a fault is over, while the child is yet so young as to be merely under the government of instinct and impulse, that is, perhaps, till the age of five years. There are, indeed, sometimes cases in which a child appears fixed in a state of sullenness or passive rebellion, from causes that are mainly physical, and refuses to obey chiefly from the difficulty of rousing itself out of its sluggish inertness of body; too naughty to take the refreshing run in the garden which would restore its healthy action. It may then be well to rouse the physical energy by a vigorous shake, or even, in very stubborn cases, by a blow; at all events, this would be much better than serious remonstrance and lecturing, where there is no capacity or inclination to listen to it—a beating down of the mind, a moral drubbing, which may give satisfaction to the provoked inflictor, but does irremediable mischief to the bewildered victim. After reason has become so much developed as to be a habitual guiding power, when transgression has become deliberate, it may be profitable to detain a child more or less in a state of mental suffering, or deprivation of happiness; it may do him good to ponder awhile over his folly and its consequences. He will feel that he has deserved pain; he will acquiesce, or may be led to acquiesce, in his own punishment. Without this acquiescence punishment can never be otherwise than injurious. It will appear merely as a tyrannical power and vengeance, and will stimulate all angry and revengeful feelings in return. As soon as the parent appears in this light of a tyrant, his moral power is lost. Rebellion, or, worse still, slavish, cowardly obedience, will ensue. He must be recognized by the child as only the administrator of the Divine law of retribution, which is written upon his own conscience, and then no evil feeling will result —no permanent evil feeling, even though the human infirmity of the parent should lead him to undue severity.

MANNERS.

Few persons in these days are so cynical as to maintain that manners are of no consequence. Though they are but the external surface of character, and therefore not of the vital importance which belongs to the inner life and root of it, still it would be absurd to deny that the qualities of that surface do very much concern the happiness both of the individual and of society. If beauty alone were in question, the outward grace of manner would deserve and repay such sedulous care. The gardener's labor is not spent in vain when he cherishes into bloom merely the brilliant-tinted flower. The wise cultivator of the human plant, however, will bear in mind the analogy of nature, and will not think he can produce that beauty by painting the surface. If art can add a tint to the flower, it must be by laying no pigment on the petal, but by infusing a new chemical element into the soil, which must ascend through the pores of the stem, and be elaborated in its secret glands. And so to cultivate manners that will be really attractive, we must labor from the soul of man outward, and they in their turn will re-act upon the inner life and aid the growth and development of virtuous character; as those flowers and leaves with their polished surfaces imbibing the sun and air give back nourishment to root and stem.

Good manners should be cultivated because, first, they *are* good; they are beautiful, suitable, proper;

they gratify the artistic perception in ourselves; a refined mind would prompt to elegant action in a solitary wilderness; in the second place, because they are agreeable to others, and to give pleasure is no mean branch of benevolence. Let the best motives be present to the mind of the teachers and the taught, and the work will be incomparably best performed. Let children be trained to sit quietly, to talk gently, to eat with nicety, to salute gracefully, to help another before themselves, because it is *proper*, it is kind, it is becoming to do so; not because Mrs. Grundy will stare at them and think them naughty if they do otherwise. It is best of all to behave prettily, because it *is* pretty; it is well to behave prettily, because it will please Mrs. Grundy; the lowest motive, which leads to merely artificial and counterfeit elegance, is to behave prettily because Mrs. Grundy will think it pretty.

Politeness, which Johnson describes to be "the never giving any preference to oneself," frequently, we know, lies all upon the surface; still, this is better than the absence of it; for, as we have already intimated, the habitual regard to observances which are prescribed upon the principles of benevolence, which is at the root of all politeness and good manners, will lead by degrees to the love and practice of benevolence itself. And when it is considered how contagious are all the feelings of our nature, whether good or evil—how the frown will excite an answering frown, as smiles will kindle smiles—how the rude jest will provoke the insolent reply—how he that always takes care of number one, will find himself jostled by a host of equally independent units, whose bristles are roused in emulation of his own—it is evident that the well-being of society is affected in no slight degree by the regard which is paid to the outward decencies and amenities of life. Manners may not now mean morals, but they are the best possible substitute.

EXAMPLE.

We must here again repeat the great rule in education: Be yourself what you wish your children to be; or to express it more practically, Be yourself under the guidance of the same principles as those by which you would guide your children. There may be natural reasons why a parent can not in all things be a pattern for his children—besides difference in age there may be infirmities and deficiences over which he has no control; besides which, they may be differently constituted, so that the rule which is right for him may not be applicable to them. In the striving, then, after excellence, rather than in any condition of Being actually attained, he must be an example to his children, and never, through any false idea of maintaining his authority, inspiring reverence—in short, humoring his own pride, attempt to concentrate their view on himself as their beau ideal, and so heap a weight of responsibility on his own head which he is naturally incapable of sustaining.

The duty, then, of parents in the matter of example is twofold. To make right principles living realities, by their own obedience to them, and to gain such an attractive power over the minds of their children, that they, too, shall be brought into the same subservience.

It does not necessarily follow that children should

imitate their parents or instructors: they will invariably imitate those who most forcibly fix their attention. A mother or governess may be most wise, most virtuous, most everything, but if there happen to be in the nursery or neighborhood any who will amuse their fancy with marvelous stories, answer all their questions, and invent fascinating games, these geniuses will be, in the child's judgment, authorities of a much higher order than the keepers of the law in the parlor. Superiority of mind in itself, and the tendency to quietness and reflection which the possession of knowledge gives, often add much to the indisposition of grown-up persons to amuse children in their own way; and a romping nursemaid will, therefore, soon obtain a hold over them which the mother fails to do. Whoever can make children the happiest will have the most influence over them, and it is much easier to make them happy by exciting their animal spirits than by interesting them mentally. Persons of coarse, uneducated minds, generally appeal directly to these animal feelings in their efforts to amuse children, and will draw away affection and influence from the careful instructors who try to make progress by delicate and less exciting means. Parents, then, must learn the art of inspiring interest in the pursuits which they themselves direct, and there must be such happy associations with all the intercourse between them and their children, that no gratifications which can be procured from other sources shall really have a counteracting charm.

It is piteous sometimes to see what a dull place the drawing-room is made to a child, and how it must soon learn to dislike the society of its parents and their friends. So long as it sits quietly and makes no noise and looks like a little block of wood, it is called a good child, and perhaps overwhelmed with kisses—that is to say, commended for being inanimate and indolent, and for making no use of its faculties. But as soon as it begins to grow restless, to pull about everything within reach, and to urge eagerly, and perhaps noisily, oft-repeated questions concerning the nature and reason of this thing and that, the bell is rung, the child is considered a nuisance and given to the servant; and while it is almost bursting with shame and disappointment, which it can only express by cries and sobs, "naughty child" is reiterated, and it is again banished to the nursery. It is, in fact, punished for being happy, for employing its powers, for making its own best efforts for expanding its little mind; and precisely at the moment when the faculties are in the best possible state for receiving right impressions, they are checked; bad feelings are excited, and it is sent among those who may perhaps misunderstand its wishes, and thwart or punish its anxious desire to *know;* leaving the poor child with a deep and bitter sense of unjust treatment.

It is granted that children must not talk and be troublesome in company; and one use of a nursery and garden is to prevent this. There they may have full play to work off the animal effervescence in active games and bodily exercise of all sorts, and the quieter amusements should be reserved for the parlor. A supply of little occupations, adapted to his capacity and made interesting by the explanation and occasional participation of his elders, are the best preventives to the restlessness which makes a child troublesome. And whenever a child can amuse himself without interfering with the comfort of others, it seems a pity that he should be kept to the nursery. The little creature is constantly imbibing, sideways, so to speak, a portion of all he hears and sees, and his character is fed every instant by the atmosphere of habits and ideas around him. Can we, then, be too cautious with whom we place the child in contact? Surely not; and yet must we not say that, in ordinary cases, nursemaids, often ignorant, and with selfish feelings decidedly predominant, are the chief companions of the young in early childhood? Easy, indolent mothers think themselves fortunate when they have a nursemaid who amuses the children well and keeps them happy all the day long without any trouble to herself; it is so much burden off her shoulders. She is a little annoyed, certainly, to discover that they have caught the nurse's grammar and accent, and, perhaps, sets herself to work to correct this with much vigilance. She does not consider, that when she has succeeded in laying a fine coat of varnish on the surface, the tone of thought and feeling which has been imbibed deeper down lies entirely untouched. In fact, in proportion as the children are made happy out of her sight, she must be careful to watch over their moral growth, because, as was said before, a child's heart opens immediately to receive impressions from any one who makes him happy.

But if it be granted that our nursemaids are inefficient, do we find that mothers, even among the higher classes, are usually adequate to their office? If we look but to the education, the training, which young ladies commonly receive—to their course of life at that period of existence when they ought to be qualifying themselves for the important trust which may hereafter devolve upon them—the question answers itself. What part of their studies or pursuits bears any direct relation to the responsibility they take upon themselves? They come to the task ignorant of the anatomy, the physiology, the mental constitution of the young being whose charge devolves upon them, and of all the most important provisions for insuring its health and happiness. Engaged in the frivolous pursuits of the world, introduced into society at an early age, dressing, dancing, visiting; when they are called to the most momentous duties, they are obliged to rely upon an ignorant nurse, to trust to old women's tales, for what ought to have been correct knowledge. It is a fortunate circumstance in this case if the mother has sense enough to know her own unfitness and to delegate the office to some one who is qualified; but if she has true reason to believe that she possesses the gift of making children happy, and of guiding and governing them well at the same time, it ought only to be strict necessity that prevents her being their chief and almost constant companion. Those children are much privileged who believe their mother to be a treasure of all excellence as well as their own best friend, and if she can gain by fair means such a compliment as a little girl of three years old paid her mamma, "You are the bestest and beautifullest of all," she will rejoice at it, and turn the conviction to good account, whatever hallucination there may be in the matter.

Teaching by bad example we believe to be a fatal error. It is often maintained that young people—that is, boys or young men—should be made acquainted with the world and its wickedness, in order that they may avoid it: as the Spartans exposed their drunken Helots to teach sobriety. This is a very dangerous experiment. Custom and example have always a tendency to become stronger than morality and principle. Under strong temptation, the mere knowledge that a thing has been done, or is done, weakens resistance, and the first step in vice is thus made more easy. After the first step, the road presents few obstacles. Keep the mind pure and in ignorance of the ways and wickedness of the world, in early life at least, until the principles are fixed and the vision clear enough to see distinctly where the road leads to.

SECTION III.

ON THE CONNECTION OF MIND WITH ORGANIZATION—THE SUBJECTIVE AND THE OBJECTIVE.

THE Brain is the organ of Mind; it is not a single organ, but many, manifesting a plurality of faculties; and vigor of function, other things being the same, is in proportion to the quality, health, and size of the organ. It has hitherto been too much the practice to consider that Education is everything, and original constitution nothing; that mind is a sort of *tabula rasa* on which anything may be written by a careful and judicious training; but this is only true to a certain extent. Education can do much, but it can not compensate for or supply the want arising from original natural deficiency. How much depends upon ourselves, that is, upon original constitution, which the Germans call the subjunctive element, and how much upon education, or the objective, has never yet been marked with sufficient definiteness in works on Education. In the region of the Intellect, it is true that extraordinary natural powers of mental calculation and mathematical and musical and artistic talents have been observed, and also the equally marked absence of these faculties; but the differences in our natural powers of feeling, if equally marked, have been less observed and insisted upon. It is very generally admitted that the lover's feeling is subjective, that is, has its source in himself, and not in the object; and that the *perfection* which the mother sees in her infant darling and all its pretty ways, is in herself, and not in the child; these feelings being strong in proportion as Amativeness and Philoprogenitiveness are well developed; but it is not equally apparent with respect to the higher feelings of our nature, that a man feels justly or kindly, not in proportion to his familiarity with the truths of Christianity, but as the parts of the brain connected with Conscientiousness and Benevolence are large or small. It is not what we know, but what we feel, that usually regulates our conduct; and if what we feel depends upon the size of the parts of the brain with which the feelings are connected, it is useless to deceive ourselves by expecting from people more than their organization warrants. If the selfish feelings predominate, it is useless to expect other than a selfish person, or a superior kind of animal; the moral feelings, though weak, may restrain the propensities within the limits of law—common courtesy and politeness and a good education may enable an individual to seem to the world all that the world requires; but yet the character at its base is, and will continue, essentially selfish. Where the animal or selfish and the other feelings are equally balanced, then education and existing circumstances or companionship will determine which shall predominate. Society, as it at present exists, is organized principally upon the predominance of the selfish feelings, and ascends in feeling little above the self-regarding organs of Self-esteem and Approbativeness. Each person is expected as his first, if not his sole, duty to take care of himself. The Christian virtues are worn more for ornament than for use, and a selfish person is more in harmony with things around him than those in whom the higher feelings predominate. It is difficult, then, in ordinary society to distinguish one class of persons from the other. Although in the home-circle the really selfish character is generally recognizable, yet circumstances may not arise even in a lifetime to test such character before the world or even to friends. As we have said before, custom, society, education, aided by Approbativeness, will enable every one to talk the language of all the feelings, but the first trial would probably show that all the feelings were by no means strong enough to influence the conduct.

As an illustration, how often do we find such persons warm in their expressions of friendship toward the prosperous, but equally cool and cautious as regards linking themselves by any ties whatever with the unfortunate; extremely ready to disapprove and blame in the day of adversity, or at the best to quietly walk away, leaving a fair field for the offices of friendship to those always unobtrusive, and frequently, therefore, less noticed persons, whose moral feelings are strong as their moral organs are well developed. If the organ of Conscientiousness is very deficient, there may be great natural kindness of heart and strong religious feeling, but there will be as great a moral blindness as there is physical blindness where the eyes are closed; and so of the æsthetic feelings, where they are absent, the mind is closed to the perception of beauty, of perfection, and of poetry. Education can really do very little to compensate or correct nature's short-comings. It is of no use ignoring these truths; it is much better to know what we are—our weakness as well as strength—so that we may not overrate our powers, and the blind lead the blind into the ditch.

The difference in the powers of thought are equally great with those of feeling. The objects of knowledge are ideas. Ideas, however, are not purely subjective or formed within ourselves. Something without ourselves which we call matter or the object—but of whose nature or essence we know nothing—acts upon the sense, the sense upon the intellectual faculty, and the faculties are connected with different organs of the brain, the vigor of function, or the strength and vividness of the ideas, being in proportion to the size of the organs. Ideas are thus compounded equally of the object, the sense, and the intellect, and we can not resolve an idea so compounded into its elements. It has been well observed, "It is God's synthesis, and man can not undo it." We can not tell what the world is, but as it is mirrored in our minds—modified by our forms of thought—neither can thought or ideas exist, except from the action of something external to ourselves; therefore, Realism and Idealism is a vain distinction, having no foundation in *human* nature at least. Appearances *may* be entirely the *production of the mind* to which they appear, as the Idealists hold; or they may be the pure *presentation* of the things themselves, as believed by the Realists — we have no means of resolving the synthesis.

It is not the intention of the present work to enter upon the subject of the Intellectual Faculties, only so far as they are connected with the brain, and differ in relative strength in proportion to the size of their organs. Our intellectual faculties give us ideas of things or individuals, and their qualities of form, size, weight, color, order, number, and locality; they give ideas of motion or action, of comparison and causation, and of time and tune—or melody and language; and in proportion as their material organs are well-developed, are our relative powers of thought. They may be partially well-developed, giving genius in one direction; or they may be all well-developed, giving general power of mind. We have known the organ of Number so large in an idiotic boy that he could calculate faster mentally than a first-rate arithmetician could on a slate; and in the same way it may be said of all the intellectual faculties—they may be relatively well-developed, or relatively deficient. Thus Form with Constructiveness and Imitation gives a talent for drawing. Add Individuality, Color, and Ideality—it makes a portrait painter; and with the addition to these of Locality, it makes a landscape painter. If any of these organs are deficient, success in these departments must not be expected; although, unless they are very deficient, mediocrity may be attained by careful training. So of all the faculties; but there can not be a more fatal mistake than to suppose, that because the powers of the mind are strong in one direction, they are equally strong in all; what is true of the organ of Number in the idiotic calculator, may be true with respect to the other faculties in other people; some of them may be, and often are, in an idiotic state, however relatively strong and active other faculties may be. A person may thus be very learned, may read a great deal and recollect almost all he reads, may have great power of expression, both in speech and writing, and yet, for want of a full development of the reflective faculties, his judgment may be rarely sound, and his opinion on many subjects worthless. Yet the person himself is seldom conscious of this; his opinion of himself being guided by the strength of the powers he has and the relative development of his Self-esteem; neither is the world generally any wiser, for its opinion is influenced by his learning and the noise he is able to make with it. There is an old proverb, however, used by Chaucer, which says: "The greatest clerks are not always the wisest men." It is asserted by Dr. Wilson, the author of a very elaborate work on the subject, and confirmed, we believe, by Dr. Brewster, that as large a proportion as one person in every eighteen is color-blind in some marked degree, and that one in every fifty-five confounds red with green. This is owing to the small size of the organ of Color, and all the other organs are liable to be relatively as imperfect. Yet few, we are told, are conscious of their color-blindness; and fewer still admit that there can be any defect in any other departments of their mental vision, or that they are not quite as capable, naturally, of judging upon all subjects as the most perfect organizations around them.

The world, then, may be said to be manufactured within us with a perfection and vividness proportionate to the size and quality of our organs, and to no two persons, therefore, can it possibly appear alike, inasmuch as the organizations of no two persons are alike. "The eye sees only what it brings with it the power to see," both by natural power and cultivation; and as we all differ in feeling as well as in intellectual capacity, it is sheer arrogance to dogmatize and lay down the law for others. A wise man will know that it is impossible for him to say more than how *he* feels, or *how things appear to him*, on any subject; and to *insist* upon other people feeling and thinking the same, is mere folly.

In estimating the effect of the organization through which the mind acts, almost as much depends upon quality or temperament as upon the size of the organ, and there is as much difference in nervous susceptibility between individuals of the same race, size, and form as between the thick-skinned rhinoceros and the fiery and excitable race-horse. Genius, in particular directions, may be caused by the extraordinary size of particular organs; but genius generally results from the superior natural degree of cerebral excitability. The power of correct appreciation, of creation, of imagination—the inspirations of the poet and the madman—are but different degrees of exaltation of the same faculties—different temperings of the same spring:

> "The lunatic, the lover, and the poet,
> Are of imagination all compact!"

says Shakespeare. Plato says: "The greatest blessings we have spring from madness, when granted by Divine bounty." It is evident he means, when arising from exalted temperament; for he says: "He who without the madness of the Muses approaches the gates of poesy, under the persuasion that by means of art he can become an efficient poet, doth himself fail in his purpose and his poetry, being that of a sane man; he is thrown into the shade by the poetry of such as are mad."

"We do not hear that Memnon's statue gave forth its melody at all under the rushing of the mightiest wind, or in response to any other influence, divine or human, than certain short-lived sunbeams of morning; and we must learn to accommodate ourselves to the discovery that some of those cunningly-fashioned instruments called human souls (dependent in this life both on organization and temperament), have only a very limited range of music, and will not vibrate in the least under a touch that fills others with tremulous rapture or quivering agony." *

Admitting, then, that vigor of function is in proportion to the health and size of the material organ with which the mind is connected, and that although education may do much, still more depends upon the perfection of the instrument, the deductions from these premises are of obvious importance.

Education we have defined to be "the developing and perfecting of all the faculties which make a complete man," and the first requisite is a large and healthy and well-formed brain. Education here must begin before birth, for much depends upon the mental and bodily constitution of the parents. Important as this is, little attention has yet been paid to it. What little knowledge we have on this subject has been hitherto devoted to the animal creation. Marriages are made with reference to almost every circumstance but the healthy mental constitution of the offspring. If a license be procured, Providence is supposed to take care of all the rest; and yet we are required to study God's laws and to act in accordance with them as much in this department as in all others; and, in fact, we may say be-

---

* Adam Bede.

fore all others, if we would advance rapidly toward true humanity. Miraculous intervention will no more save us here than elsewhere from the effects of our own ignorance and folly. Biography shows that most men of note in the world have owed much of their celebrity to their mothers, who have all been remarkable in their sphere.

Another essential point to be observed in relation to the connection of mind with organization, is that the brain develops itself in a given order; certain parts arriving at maturity before others. The selfish or animal feelings and the perceptive faculties come first to maturity, next the moral feelings, and last of all the reasoning powers are developed. We should, in consequence, be very careful not to overwork any part of the brain or mental faculty which is but imperfectly developed. Great and serious mischief has arisen, and is constantly arising, from the neglect of this law, and from ignorance of the gradual steps by which our faculties are unfolded; it should be our effort, therefore, to assist, and not to force their growth by giving them more exercise than their immature state will bear.

Dr. Caldwell, in his valuable work on Physical Education, observes: "Parents are often too anxious that their children should have a knowledge of the alphabet, of spelling, reading, geography, and other branches of school-learning at a very early age. This is worse than tempting them to walk too early, because the organ likely to be injured by it is much more important than the muscles and bones of the lower extremities. It may do irreparable mischief to the brain. That viscus is yet too immature and feeble to sustain fatigue. Until from the sixth to the eighth year of life, the seventh being, perhaps, the proper medium, all its energies are necessary for its own healthy development and of that of the other portions of the system. Nor ought they to be directed by *serious study* to any other purpose. True, exercise is as essential to the health and vigor of the brain at that time of life as at any other; but it should be the *general and pleasurable exercise of observation and action.* It ought not to be the compulsory exercise of tasks. Early prodigies of mind rarely attain mature distinction. The reason is plain; their brains are injured by premature toil, and their general health impaired. From an unwise attempt to convert at once their flowery spring into a luxuriant summer, that summer too often never arrives. The blossom withers ere the fruit is formed."

Parents, then, must be satisfied to wait for the effects of the best regulated system of training until all the faculties are matured. If a child of early age be selfish, it is not a sufficient reason for its continuance in selfishness after the period when the moral feelings, owing to greater physical advancement, act with greater strength; neither if a child be dull and stupid, intellectually considered, is it necessary that he should remain so after the period when the reasoning powers are fully developed. We can not look for the full fruits of judicious mental cultivation until after fifteen or sixteen years of age, when all the feelings and mental faculties will generally have attained to a fair degree of their natural growth and strength. The process of training which we have advocated for children may not be so easy as the consigning them early to school; but if parents can resolve to undertake so much present trouble—and surely they ought not to shrink from it—if they will work slowly and patiently, and not expect to reap at once the fruits of their labors, they may reckon upon a harvest which in future years shall recompense their cares a hundredfold.

An important result of the union of the mind with organization is the influence of the passions—of each feeling or group of feelings—upon the health of the body, and upon the duration of life, as well as upon our habitual cheerfulness and happiness. It is the characteristic of the propensities or selfish feelings never to be satisfied; and, as to produce the same excitement, the drunkard is obliged each day to increase the dram, so all our propensities, Ambition, Love of Power, Love of Acquisition, etc., crave increased excitement to produce the same pleasure; until at last, with advanced age, such sources of enjoyment fail, and they who have trusted to them find, with Solomon, that " all is vanity and vexation of spirit." This is the most favorable course of the selfish feelings when successful and pleasurably excited; but when unsuccessful in their aims, and painfully excited, then they seem to diffuse a poison throughout the whole system, to darken the mind and impair the bodily health. Unsuccessful love, betrayed or slighted friendship, blighted ambition, etc., and the host of ill-feelings and passions they raise up, such as envy, hatred, malice, jealousy, anger, fear, grief, all act injuriously on the bodily system. Each passion or sentiment has its own way of affecting the body, as it is painfully or pleasurably excited. Pale with fear, sick with love, and other similar modes of expression are not merely metaphorical, any more than affections of the heart, bowels of compassion, the breathlessness of surprise, and others; but are all truly indicative of parts or functions of the body intimately affected by mental states. The circulation, the digestion, the heart, the liver, the kidneys, are all influenced and disturbed under the excitement of passion or strong emotion. These functions also, when disturbed, *re-act* upon the mind. Thus, Dr. Reid says: " He whose disposition to goodness can resist the influence of dyspepsia, and whose career of philanthropy is not liable to be checked by an obstruction in the hepatic [liver] organs, may boast of much deeper and firmer virtue than falls to the ordinary lot of human nature." The propensities are all liable to increase in activity till they become passions, and the temperature of passion is too hot to allow of the existence, much less the growth and healthy development of the numerous small, quiet, but not the less necessary daily virtues. Any object of desire, when such desire amounts to passion—the etymology of which word is suffering—whether successful or unsuccessful, wears both mind and body. Hope and fear are then alternatively so strong that we may bid farewell to all mental tranquillity; and when want of success brings disappointment, health gives way, and the springs of life are poisoned :

> "Thus the warm youth,
> Whom love deludes into his thorny wilds,
> Through flowery, tempting paths, or leads a life
> Of fevered rapture, or of cruel care ;
> His brightest aims extinguished all, and all
> His lively moments running down to waste."
> —THOMSON.

On the contrary, a very different state of both body and mind attends the activity of the unselfish feelings. When they habitually predominate, a constant and almost unvarying cheerfulness is the result—a cheerfulness which no grief or trouble or misfortune can long depress. Mind and body then work smoothly together, and the good or bad events that fortune brings upon us are felt according to the qualities that *we*, not *they*, possess. The subjective or internal overpowers the objective or external, and such persons are said to be constitutionally happy. Poets and philosophers all bear witness to this habitually sunshiny cast of mind; thus, Pope says:

> "What nothing earthly gives, or can destroy,
> The soul's calm sunshine and the heartfelt joy,
> Is virtue's prize."

" Love, hope, and joy," says Haller, " promote perspiration, quicken the pulse, promote the circulation, increase the appetite, and facilitate the cure of diseases." " A constant serenity, supported by hope or cheerfulness arising from a good conscience, is the most healthful of all affections of the mind," says Dr. Mackenzie; and again, Dr. Sweetzer says: " Let me remark, that all those mental avocations which are founded in benevolence, or whose end or aim are the good of mankind, being from their very nature associated with agreeable moral excitement, and but little mingled with the evil feelings—as envy, jealousy, hatred—must necessarily diffuse a kindly influence throughout the constitution."

If, then, we trust to find our happiness in the indulgence of the selfish feelings, even if successful in our aims, the happiness is but transient; and as life advances we find only vacuity or disappointment, and our way to the tomb is cold, dark, joyless, and merely vegetative. On the contrary, where the moral, the æsthetic, the religious feelings have been duly cultivated and predominate, happiness, not so intense, but more enduring—calm, tranquil, and serene—increases as we grow older; passion has ceased, the propensities are all quiet or under due control; health and contentment reign in body and mind; and at last, in the " soul's calm sunshine," we fall asleep.

The object, then, of moral training is the habitual predominance and activity of the higher and unselfish feelings; and we can not begin this most important portion of education too early.

SECTION IV.

THE EDUCATION OF THE INTELLECTUAL FACULTIES.

The education of the Intellectual faculties is no part of the object of the present work. I shall make, therefore, only two or three remarks that appear to us of considerable importance.

Memory, Imagination, Perception, Conception, Judgment, are not primitive mental faculties, but mere modes of action of all the primitive faculties, and the intellect can only be properly trained by appealing to the primitive faculties themselves. If all the mental faculties were cultivated in the same direct way and with the same assiduity as Tune, we should soon see a different result to the one usually attained.

We must be careful not to lose the end of the cultivation of the intellect in the means we take to acquire it. Thus, as Mr. Combe says, we must have "an early conviction that man is made for action; that he is placed in a theater of agents, which he must direct, or to which he must accommodate his conduct; that everything in the world is regulated by laws instituted by the Creator; that all objects that exist, animate and inanimate, have received definite qualities and constitutions, and that good arises from their proper, and evil from their improper, application." These are the proper objects or ends of knowledge, and it must always be borne in mind that reading, writing, arithmetic, languages, and mathematics, disconnected from their application to realities, though highly useful in exercising the mental faculties and in preparing the mind to receive knowledge, are not *knowledge*, but the mere instruments of acquiring it, and it is only in such a light that they should be regarded. If a boy's time and attention be engrossed by the acquisition of these mere instruments of learning, as has been too much the case hitherto, it is likely he may lose all taste for the knowledge which they are to fit him for acquiring. Let him be introduced into the kingdom of nature itself, and he will imbibe a taste for and love of knowledge, which will always remain with him, and which will make him eager to acquire the means of obtaining it.

The mind having become acquainted with the external things — their properties, their relations; being stored with the facts of natural history and science; having observed the various operations that are going on — physical, chemical, and vital; it will begin to inquire into their causes, and the reflective powers will come into more especial operation. The study of science may now be entered upon, the knowledge acquired arranged under its proper heads, and each fact placed in the department to which it belongs. A clear and concise arrangement for this purpose has been given by Dr. Arnott, in the "Table of Science," contained in the Introduction to his "Physics." It is of great consequence that both teachers and pupils should carry in their minds a clear conception of the general field of human knowledge, and of the comparative importance of its several subdivisions; and perhaps, as he affirms,

REV. JOSEPH COOK.
INTELLECTUAL FACULTIES.

PLATE XXVIII.

this is the most valuable single acquirement that the mind can make. It is because I am so decidedly of this opinion that I have introduced any allusion to the Intellect in this work. The field of knowledge gets larger and larger, and young minds start without any chart for their guidance through the weary waste. It is most important to all further attainments that we should first possess ourselves of the simple fundamental principles in all the great departments of science. Dr. Arnott's table enables us to get a clear view of where these are to be found; we shall therefore give it here, with the substance of the valuable remarks attached to it:

TABLE OF SCIENCE.

1. Physics.
Mechanics,
Hydrostatics,
Hydraulics,
Pneumatics,
Acoustics,
Heat,
Optics,
Electricity,
Astronomy,
   etc.

2. Chemistry.
Simple substances.
Mineralogy,
Geology,
Pharmacy,
Brewing,
Dyeing,
Tanning,
   etc.

3. Life.
Vegetable Physiology,
Botany,
Horticulture,
Agriculture,
   etc.

4. Mind.
Intellect.
Reasoning,
Logic,
Language,
Education,
   etc.

	Motives to Action.
Animal Physiology,	Emotions and Passions,
Zoology,	Justice,
Anatomy,	Morals,
Pathology,	Government,
Medicine,	Political economy,
etc.	etc.
	Natural Theology.

5. SCIENCE OF QUANTITY.

Arithmetic,   Algebra,   Geometry,   etc.

"Supposing *description of particulars* or *Natural History*, to be studied along with the different parts of the *System of Science* sketched in the table, there will be included in the scheme the whole knowledge of the universe which man can acquire by the exercise of his own powers; that is to say, which he can acquire independently of a supernatural *Revelation*. And on this knowledge all his arts are founded; some of them on the single part of Physics, as that of the machinist, architect, mariner, carpenter, etc.; some on Chemistry (which includes Physics), as that of the miner, glass-maker, dyer, brewer, etc.; and some on Physiology (which includes much of Physics and Chemistry), as that of the scientific gardener or botanist, agriculturist, zoologist, etc. The business of teachers of all kinds, and of governors, advocates, linguists, etc., respects chiefly the science of mind. The art of medicine requires in its professor a comprehensive knowledge of all the departments.

"As the sciences are all intimately connected with each other, great advantage must result from studying them in the order above given—for *Chemistry* can not be well understood without a previous knowledge of *Physics;* and *Life*, consisting of Animal and Vegetable Physiology, is a superstructure on the other two, and can not be studied independently of them. This method of proceeding, therefore, will prevent repetitions and anticipations, and considerably diminish the labor of acquirement.

"It thus appears that the *Science of Nature* may be considered as a continuous and closely-connected system of history, which, to be clearly understood, must be studied according to the natural order of its parts, just as any common history must be read in the natural order of its paragraphs. But so little has this been known, or at least acted upon, in general, that perhaps no other human plans, formed with one object, have been so dissimilar and inconsistent as the common plans of education.

"The notions on education prevalent in the world until recently, have been as erroneous with respect to the comparative importance of different branches of knowledge as with respect to the order of study. Thus, at many of our famed Schools, and even Universities, the attention has been directed almost exclusively either to *Languages* and *Logic*, or to *Abstract Mathematics;* the preceptors seeming to forget that these objects have no value but in their application to Physics, Chemistry, Life, and Mind. The reason for bestowing much attention on the Greek and Roman languages was good some centuries ago, because then no book of value existed which was not written in one of these languages; but now the case is completely reversed, for he who learns almost any matter of science from old books is learning error, or, at the least, knowledge far short of modern erudition. As to the higher mathematics, again, while they merit great honor, as being the instrument by which many useful discoveries have been made, and the conjectures of powerful minds have been confirmed, still, a very deep investigation of them is neither possible to the generality of men, nor, if it were so, would it be of utility. The mode of proceeding, then, to which we have alluded, is just as if a man to whom permission were given to enter and use a magnificent garden, on condition of his procuring a key to open the gate, and certain measures to estimate the riches contained within, should waste his whole life on the road in polishing one key and procuring others of different materials and workmanship, or in preparing a multiplicity of unnecessary measures. This and many similar errors arise from persons not being in general taught to carry in their minds a clear conception of the general field of human knowledge, and so of the comparative importance of the different subdivisions—the possession of which conception is perhaps the most valuable single acquirement which the mind can make. He whose view is bounded by the limits of one or two small departments, will probably have very false ideas even of them, but he certainly will of other parts, and of the whole; so as to be constantly exposed to commit errors hurtful to himself or to others. His mind, compared to the well-ordered mind of a properly educated man, is what the misshapen body of a mechanic, crippled by his trade, is to the body of the active mountaineer or other specimen of perfect human nature.

"We now proceed to remark, that by arranging science according to its natural relations, and therefore so as to avoid repetitions and anticipations, a very complete system might be exhibited in small bulk, viz, in five volumes, of which the separate titles would be, 1st, *Physics ;* 2d, *Chemistry ;* 3d, *Organic Life*, or *Physiology ;* 4th, *Mind ;* and, 5th, *Measures* or *Mathematics.* From such works, with less trouble than it now costs to obtain familiarity with one new language, a man might obtain a general acquaintance with science. And such is the close relation of the departments of science with each other, that consummate skill in any one may generally be acquired more easily, by first studying the whole in a general way, and then applying particularly to that one, than by fixing the attention from the beginning upon the one more exclusively. The study of Anatomy thus becomes very easy to him who has first studied Physics.

"Were such elementary treatises once in existence, they might be maintained complete by a periodical incorporation of new discoveries; and if furnished with correct and copious references, they might form an index to the whole existing mass of knowledge. This *Book of Nature* would be of more value to the world than any other conceivable institution for education, for it would convert the minds of millions into intellectual organs of advancement; while in the crowd, many would probably be found in every age as highly endowed by nature as any that have yet appeared along the extended stream of time."

It is scarcely possible that an individual thus introduced to the world and to himself should not acquire a taste for knowledge and a thirst for information. The principles of science are now so much simplified that they may be made comprehensible even to ordinary understandings, and neither sex should be excluded from the intellectual tastes and enjoyments to which such knowledge must lead.

The *Science* of *Physics*, or *Natural Philosophy*, explains the causes of the phenomena of the material world, and furnishes never-failing subjects of interesting inquiry; all the ordinary occupations of life, all that is going on in the world of nature around us, are, in fact, series of experiments in Natural Philosophy, which may be explained and made interesting to children at a very early age. The reasoning powers may be thus directed to all the changes that are going on around us, the causes of most of which are easy of explanation, and may be illustrated without difficulty by simple experiments.

Chemistry shows us how all the different kinds of matter go to form the endless variety of substances on the face of the earth.

Life introduces us to the animal and vegetable kingdoms, with their different divisions and classifications. It explains the principles of vegetation, and gives to the garden, to the flowery mead, and to every hedge and bank a tenfold interest. It introduces us to the wonderful structure of our own frames, to that of animals and their comparative anatomy, to the laws of health, to all the phenomena of sensation, self-motion, growth, decay, death, etc., and to all that we as yet know of their causes.

The *Science of Quantity*, or *Mathematics*, gives us

rules for applying the measures or standards that express quantity, and for comparing all kinds of quantities with each other.

The study of *Mind*, the most important of all, introduces us to ourselves; it makes known to us our feelings and intellectual faculties—their character and nature; the end they are intended to answer, *i. e.*, their use, and it also explains their abuse; it shows their proper and legitimate sphere of action, and the relation they bear to things and circumstances; and, ultimately, how they may all be used so as to insure to their possessor the largest return of happiness of which his nature is capable. This knowledge is simple, as we have endeavored to show in the foregoing part of this work, and may early be brought home to the mind of a child; he may be made to understand the nature of his faculties; he may be led to see clearly the distinction between the selfish feelings and those that tend to the happiness of others, and thus learn to analyze the motives of his actions, and become ashamed of such as are purely selfish. No kind of knowledge can be so calculated to prevent the abuse of the faculties, and to assist the teacher in moral training, as such a knowledge of self.

This is a sketch of the education which the Intellectual Faculties must receive, if we would exercise them all and upon their proper objects. In this manner the nature and properties of things—their relation to ourselves and happiness—will be learned, and in a manner that can not fail of being pleasurable rather than painful and compulsory. Dr. Arnott beautifully observes, with reference to the department of Physics:

"The greatest sum of knowledge acquired with the least trouble is, perhaps, that which comes with the study of the few simple truths of Physics. To the man who understands these, very many phenomena, which to the uninformed appear prodigies, are only beautiful illustrations of his fundamental knowledge; and this he carries about with him, not as an oppressive weight, but as a charm supporting the weight of other knowledge, and enabling him to add to his valuable store every new fact of importance which may offer itself. With such a principle of arrangement, his information, instead of resembling loose stones or rubbish thrown together in confusion, becomes as a noble edifice, of correct proportions and firm contexture, and is acquiring greater strength and consistency with the experience of every succeeding day. It has been a common prejudice that persons thus instructed in general laws, had their attention too much divided and could know nothing perfectly. But the very reverse is true; for general knowledge renders all particular knowledge more clear and precise. The ignorant man may be said to have charged his hundred hooks of knowledge—to use a rude simile—with single objects; while the informed man makes each support a long chain, to which thousands of kindred and useful things are attached. The laws of Philosophy may be compared to keys which give admission to the most delightful gardens that fancy can picture; or to a magic power which unveils the face of the universe and discloses endless charms of which ignorance never dreams. The informed man, in the world, may be said to be always surrounded by what is known and friendly to him, while the ignorant man is as one in a land of strangers and enemies. A man reading a thousand volumes of ordinary books as agreeable pastime, will receive only vague impressions; but he who studies the methodized *Book of Nature*, converts the great universe into a simple and sublime history, which tells of God, and may worthily occupy his attention to the end of his days."

CONCLUSION.

It has been the endeavor of this work to associate the rules of practical education with the principles of what we believe to be the truest philosophy of the human mind that has yet been obtained. Phrenology, it is true, is yet an imperfect science. In its details it has yet to undergo many corrections; it needs much of expansion, and much of simplification. We believe, however, that its delineation of the powers of the mind is so faithful and comprehensive, that it may legitimately be made the basis of a system of education. And we are most desirous of communicating our own strong conviction that the main doctrine of Phrenology—namely, that the mind is connected with the organization of the brain, and is strong, both in intellect and feeling, in proportion as the brain is perfect, and that, consequently, the mind can only be improved by improving the cerebral organization—is essential to a right understanding of the work of education. This work can never be effectually performed till every one of the faculties of the mind receives its distinct exercise and cultivation; the knowledge of the anatomy of the mind is as necessary to every parent and instructor as that of the body to the physical operator. It is of little use to treat vaguely of the metaphysical subtleties of the Will, the Memory, the Imagination. We must penetrate to the elements of which the human character is constituted, that we may afford to each that peculiar kind of nourishment and exercise by which alone these individual functions can be developed. If human beings were all born according to the type of perfect humanity, one rule of education would apply to all; the same spiritual food would be assimilated by each, and nourish him to the full measure of his mental stature. But we know that infants are born with the miserable consequences of the sins of their progenitors stamped upon their constitutions. Minds are crippled and distorted as well as limbs, and as it would be of no use urging a child to walk if he were lame, or to see if he were blind, it is equally useless to preach the doctrines of morality and piety where there is no intellect to comprehend, nor moral nature to feel them. There are indeed the elements of that comprehension and feeling in every human being, but they may be so small and weak as to be incapable of healthy action. Must we, then, cease to preach righteousness to them? By no means; give them every chance, by placing the spiritual food within their reach, in case the stimulus of extraordinary circumstances should quicken their powers to the capacity of assimilating it; but we must at the same time act upon their lower natures by direct means of repression and encouragement adapted to the separate requirements of each of their excessive or defective organs. If there be but one portion of the brain in excess, or greatly deficient, there will be a mysterious difficulty in education, for which an experienced phrenologist will account at a glance; and surely artificial aid can be rendered more effectively with a clear knowledge of the evil than by working in the dark. Small, indeed, is the aid that can be rendered, and it is another great use of Phrenology to prevent the discouraging disappointment which attends so many benevolent, but ill-directed efforts to improve mankind.

It seems to many degrading to the mind to speak of its connection with material organization; but how can that be if it is ordained by the Divine Creator? We have only to watch and endeavor to imitate His mode of operating and not intrude our prejudices, which are the fruits of ignorance. It is seen through the whole analogy of nature that higher forms of being are developed out of lower; mind appears as the crown of creation, only associated with the greatest perfection of material organization. We do not say God *could* not have given a soul to a stone, but He has given it only to a substance of the most delicate and intricate construction. The more perfect that construction, the more perfect is the mind. What the mind is, we yet know not, nor of what development it is capable; but we know that it can grow; it can advance to higher stages of being only through the perfect action of all its present functions, as exercised through, and by means of, its material organs.

Let our efforts, then, be first directed to growing a healthy body and brain—*mens sana in sano corpore*—and when we have a healthy and strong organ, then will be time enough to set them seriously to work. It will be better that what is usually called "schooling" should not commence before ten years of age, and that there should be no steady continuous application before twelve. From twelve to fifteen or sixteen years of age, a boy will learn much better all that is required from him at school, than if his faculties had been previously tasked when they were yet in a weak and immature state. Keep children *healthy* and *happy* up to that age, and we need have no solicitude about their learning.

It will be seen that by Education we mean something very different from what is often understood by it. It is usually thought to be that which will best enable a person to get along in the world, which will make him a good man of business—clever in his profession—to the end that he may obtain wealth and place, and the consideration in society of which they are the means, without regard to the relation which these things bear to real happiness. Our object, on the contrary, is the development and proper direction of all the faculties, and especially to give the predominance to those that distinguish us from the lower animals. In proportion as our system shall tend to the advancement of the higher humanities, shall we secure the happiness of the pupil. Happiness derived solely from the propensities is not above that which the brutes enjoy. The majority of mankind seek wealth. This is their poetry and their religion; for what a man really worships—what he most reveres—is, in fact, his god. We may have all that wealth can bestow, yet, under the dominion of the propensities and merely self-regarding sentiments, we shall be constrained to confess with Solomon, that all is vanity. That there is still so much misery in the world is owing to this fact, that our aims are misdirected, and that we seek our happiness in the wrong direction. We must ascend step by step toward the development of our higher nature, and as we rise we shall become more and more independent of wealth and of the world. From the selfish and self-regarding feelings we rise to a sense of what is due to others; the requirements of our moral nature come into play; we have pleasure in our duty and in doing that which is right and kind. The next step is toward the Æsthetic; but in order to cultivate the poetry of our nature, to have a full sense of the beautiful, we must be temperate in all things, especially in mere animal gratifications; we must emancipate ourselves from the dominion of the propensities; for we must avoid all disturbing influences, and this is impossible so long as any of the lower feelings predominate. Through the Moral and the Æsthetic we reach the last step in our progress —a strong and well-directed Religious feeling. We become convinced that God is our Father, and that we have but *to learn* and *to obey*, and thence comes a Faith equal to all trial—a Faith amounting to certainty, that under the Providence of God all things must work together for good.

The great secret of happiness is constant and well-directed occupation. Enjoyments based upon the selfish feelings are always liable to fail; but when dependent upon our higher feelings, if deprived of one thing, we can always turn to another—a hundred other sources of happiness being open to us. The enjoyments from the selfish feelings grow weaker and weaker with each repetition; those from the higher, stronger and stronger; and each year thus adds to our capabilities of enjoyment. The happiness from the higher feelings is always cheap; like air, sunshine, and water, it everywhere surrounds us, for it is what *we* are—not what our circumstances are—upon which it depends. It is true, the estate may not be ours, with the care and trouble which its management entails, and the pride and vanity which its possession gratifies; but the landscape is ours, and we are spiritually in possession, if not materially. As Emerson says: "The charming landscape which I saw this morning is indubitably made up of some twenty or thirty farms. Miller owns this field, Locke that, and Manning the woodland beyond. But none of them owns the landscape. There is a property in the horizon which no man has but he whose eye can integrate all the parts—that is, the poet. This is the best part of these men's farms, yet to this their landdeeds give them no title."

> "If solid happiness we prize,
> Within our breast the jewel lies,
> And they are fools who roam."

If we would be happy, it must be in the alternate exercise of *all* our faculties upon their legitimate objects; and the Creator has placed this source of the highest happiness more within the reach of all than they who imagine it to consist in wealth—or what mere wealth can bestow—would at first suppose. It must be confessed that we rate the civilization of the present age as still low and barbaric. The great mass of mankind are still in ignorance and poverty and slavery. It is true, they are emancipated from the slavery of man to man; but they are no less the slaves of the greatest of all taskmasters—their necessities; and the majority of both rich and poor are still under the dominion of their propensities; and trusting to the selfish feelings alone, or mainly, for their happiness. From ignorance of their physical and organic structure, they are continually pushing the indulgence of such feelings beyond the bounds of health, and thus entailing numerous evils upon themselves, society, and their offspring. From the inordinate pursuit of riches, and the senseless desire of that distinction to which wealth gives birth, arise a vast load of the evils which afflict them; and while a few obtain these objects of ambition, thousands drag out a miserable existence.

But everywhere we see the dawn of a better day. On all sides are the signs of rapid development. It has taken thousands of years to arrive at our present stage, and it may perhaps take thousands more to bring man to the perfection of which his nature is capable; but hundreds will probably be sufficient to place him in a very advanced position to any which he has hitherto occupied. Let us not, however, be too sanguine, for we have to await patiently the growth of the material organs upon which the strength of the higher mental feelings depends. If all things were favorable to this growth, it must still take many generations to reach the desired point by the mass of mankind. It is not aristocratic or democratic institutions, neither monarchical nor republican, that measure progress, but this growth of the higher mental faculties. The civilization of antiquity was the advancement of the few and the slavery of the many—in Greece thirty thousand freemen and three hundred thousand slaves—and it passed away. True civilization must be measured by the progress, not of a class or nation, but of all men. God admits none to advance alone. Individuals in advance become martyrs; nations in advance, the prey of the barbarian. Only as one family of man can we make true and durable progress. But man must exist as an animal before he can exist as a man; his physical requirements must be satisfied before those of mind; and hitherto it has taken the whole time and energies of the many to provide for their physical wants. Such wants have spread mankind over the whole globe; the brute and the savage have disappeared before the superior race; the black blood of the Torrid zone has been mixed with the white of the Temperate, and a race capable of living and laboring under a zenith sun has been formed, and all seems to be preparing for a united movement onward. The elements have been pressed into our service, the powers of steam and electricity would appear boundless, and science has given man an almost unlimited control over nature. The trammels which despotism has hitherto imposed upon body and mind have been in some cases thrown off, and constitutional liberty is rapidly and widely spreading. The steamship and railway, and mutual interests in trade and commerce, have united nation to nation, and the press has ministered the progress of ideas which will tend to give one mind and simultaneous thought to the whole community. Power there is in plenty for the emancipation of the whole race; since the steam-engine and machinery may be to the working-classes what they have hitherto been to those classes above them. All that is wanted is to know how to use these forces for the general good. The powers of production are enormous; we have but to *organize them*, and justly to distribute the produce. But this can not take place under the direction of the selfish feelings alone. While we are scrambling only for individual good, physical science may advance, and our power over nature may increase, but mankind can make little progress. It is from within, now, that we must look for change; for when education, based upon correct knowledge of our constitution, shall have raised the man, there will be found no impediment to the advance of the whole race to all that is necessary for the enjoyment of the highest pleasures of which his nature is susceptible. In proportion as the higher feelings of our nature gain strength and predominate, and the law of universal brotherhood is written—is recognized in spirit, not merely upon the tongue—in proportion, in fact, as real Christianity prevails, the petty distinctions of a savage age, which form the present scale of society, will disappear, and we shall no longer seek to be distinguished by mere wealth and external advantages—gained at the expense of the excessive labor of others—but for the supremacy in us of all that distinguishes us from the brutes; for all that saves toil, instead of increasing it, and that affords time to every man for the development of· high moral and intellectual power. Distinction will be based upon worth alone, and we shall bow to an aristocracy of nature, of which the present is but the symbol. If God gives us superior abilities, we shall not glorify ourselves, but Him, and hold them in trust for the good of mankind; and wherever superior worth and talent are recognized, there will be acknowledged the future Noble—his badges not stars and garters, but the unmistakable expression of nobility which habitual obedience to that which is true and good and beautiful invariably bestows.

Everywhere in the history of the race do we trace the divine law of Progress, that makes the coarser and baser material the foundation for the finer and nobler. In the early ages of the world, man's mental state required to be fitted to his physical condition. He had the world to people and subdue; he had to compel the stubborn earth to yield him sustenance; he had to defend himself from the attacks of, and to prey in his turn upon, the animal tribes, who were its original occupiers; and it was necessary, therefore, that great activity should pervade the self-preserving organs. Hence the excess of selfishness and what is called human depravity. It would have been worse than useless to have given high moral, æsthetic, and intellectual aspirations when the sweat of the brow through the livelong day was required to supply the wants of the physical nature. Such aspirations ungratified could then, as now, only be a source of misery and discontent. As geologists show the formation of the earth to have been gradual, layer after layer being added, more perfect plants, and animals of a higher order of feeling and intelligence appearing, as the world was prepared for them—so has the mind of man been developed, region added to region, as preparation has been made for its activity and legitimate exercise. And who shall say that even the best specimen of mankind has yet reached the last development which our race is to attain even upon this earth? There appear to be rudimentary organs sufficiently developed in some individuals, when excited by mesmerism, to point to a higher order of intelligence than man has yet attained. They appear to put us in relation with the general mind of mankind; so that when steam, electricity, and machinery shall have annihilated material space and time, and when, also, we shall have made a great moral advance, it may be that these, at present, undeveloped faculties will enable us to become all-knowing and intelligent as regards what then exists, or ever has existed in the mind of man. But even if this were speculation, all history and experience—noting, as they do, an actual advance, notwithstanding much seeming local retrogression—confirm the hope that we should indulge from the nature of man himself, and point to a time when the faculties he now undoubtedly possesses being fully developed, and the powers of nature being brought to their greatest possible subservience, the earth shall become the scene of a happiness such as the imagination has hitherto conferred upon heaven alone. The very nature of man's reason, the necessity that exists for his choosing good and avoiding evil, all must act as unerringly toward his advancement, even as the laws of gravitation act to keep the earth together. Whatever is opposed to the just and good must disappear, and the kingdom of God—the empire of the true and beautiful—in the end universally prevail.

www.ingramcontent.com/pod-product-compliance
Lightning Source LLC
Chambersburg PA
CBHW031932230426
43672CB00010B/1901